MAKING A
WHITE
GARDEN

MAKING A
WHITE
GARDEN

JOAN CLIFTON

GROVE WEIDENFELD
NEW YORK

Published by Grove Weidenfeld
A division of Grove Press, Inc.
841 Broadway
New York, New York 10003–4793

First published in Great Britain in 1990 by George Weidenfeld
& Nicolson Limited, London

Library of Congress Cataloging-in-Publication Data

Clifton, Joan.
    Making a white garden / Joan Clifton. — 1st ed.
       p.   cm.
    ISBN 0–8021–1288–9 (alk. paper)
    1. Color in gardening.   2. White.   I. Title.   II. Title: White garden.
    SB454.3.C64C57   1990
    635.9′68—dc20
                                            90–37635
                                            CIP

Specially commissioned photography by Andrew Lawson

Illustrated by John Wyer

Designed by Ruth Hope

In-house designer Benn Linfield

Typeset by Keyspools Ltd., Golborne Lancs

Color separations by Newsele Litho Ltd

Printed and bound in Italy by Printers Srl, Trento

First American Edition 1990

10   9   8   7   6   5   4   3   2   1

Captions for the previous pages, front matter, and chapter openings are on page 113

Contents

Introduction

Peonies grow in such a wealth of wonderful forms and colour combinations that it is difficult to choose just a few. One essential for the shopping list is *Paeonia suffruticosa* 'Rock's Variety' with huge crumpled white petals and rich red staining set off by a mass of yellow stamens.

Texture and form have always been my first consideration when selecting plants for a garden design. I would far rather create interesting combinations of foliage shapes, using subtle contrasts of greens, yellows and greys varying in appearance from hard and shiny to soft and furry, than fill a flowerbed with a mass of competing coloured blooms. Indeed it is within such a lush, green setting that white flowers can best display their purity of form and light-reflecting qualities.

The frequently held notion that white flowers are merely 'smart', or indeed 'fashionable', entirely ignores their intense and enduring beauty and astonishing variety of form. In fact, there are white species to be found in every type of plant, whether it be a hardy shrub or a tender alpine. Petals may be thick and waxy or as fragile as tissue paper, they may be splashed with red like spilled ink,

stained with yellow blotches or open up from deep pink buds to reveal a bloom of creamy richness. Close inspection may reveal tiny green spots, delicate blue veining or fluffy orange anthers. Flowers might be huge like trumpets or composed of masses of tiny blooms like a sea of froth.

Whilst working on this book, I have become increasingly impressed by the magical qualities of white flowers and their ability to create a unique mood and atmosphere and now find my original love of these plants nearing obsession in examination of their complex variations. As I live in the centre of London, I especially appreciate their ability to transform a garden into a tranquil retreat from the busy world outside the walls.

Gertrude Jekyll was perhaps first to popularize the idea of planting schemes based on a single colour theme. Her training as a painter combined with a deep love of gardening and detailed knowledge of plant varieties enabled her to create gardens of great subtlety and charm, and her collaboration with the architect Edwin Lutyens resulted in houses and gardens which were considered, in Edwardian England, to be the ultimate in sophistication. Though many of these wonderful houses survive, the majority of their gardens have regrettably been allowed to decline, and evidence of Jekyll's creativity is mainly confined to documentary illustrations. However, one excellent example has been lovingly restored at Barrington Court in Somerset. Even more gratifying for my purposes, it contains an all-white garden which should be visited when at its most glorious, in mid-summer.

Decline and oblivion has certainly not been the fate of the famous gardens at Sissinghurst Castle in Kent. Conceived by Vita Sackville-West, they are now meticulously maintained by the National Trust. Amongst all the beautiful single-colour schemes to be found there, the exquisite white garden, so subtle and tranquil, enclosed within high boundaries has become legendary among garden lovers all over the world. Major Lawrence Johnston, another passionate plantsman of the early part of the twentieth century, devised the majestic landscape at Hidcote in Gloucester-

shire. He also worked on a [...] rooms', one of which [...] exquisite topiary work w[...]

It is my hope that by [...] and after reading thi[...] captivated by the pos[...] dening and subsequ[...] your own personal i[...] tainly is something [...] the idea of an all-w[...] draws on a su[...] ultimate in gree[...] being an unatta[...] been to make [...] practical reali[...]

Whether [...] acres or in [...] the challe[...] entirely r[...] exciting [...]

A Whiter View
Inspiration for a White Garden

White as Snow

A baby dressed in the faded ivory family christening robe, handed down from mother to daughter; a young bride resplendent in a cloud of tulle carrying a posy of white rosebuds; creamy beeswax candles flickering beside a sheaf of white lilies at the altar of a church. Somehow none of these images would be as powerful without this abundance of white.

It is as though some inner need, over which we have no control, demands that part of us is kept clear for deeper thoughts or reflections; that white can free us from the distractions and temptations of life. White represents an ideological purity.

An all-white room makes a calm and tranquil retreat; it can provide a neutral backdrop for a lively painting or a dramatic piece of sculpture. A white plate allows the unhindered presentation of the food upon it. Whites can also absorb or reflect other colours. Softly textured butter muslin curtains will take on the warm, golden hues of sunshine in the afternoon, while a white tiled floor looks blue in cold morning light.

White evokes very special images and atmosphere. Snow white – youth and innocence; ice white – coldness and calculation; white sails – freedom and movement. Moonshine white – mystery and intrigue; white tie and tails – elegance and sophistication.

The white garden can provide a perfect setting in which to recreate all these images and more; changing in mood and appearance as it moves through the seasons and as

The lily family provides a wide variety of textures amongst its dramatic white-flowering members, many of which are speckled with green yellow or orange. The thick and waxy ivory trumpets of the *Lilium* Olympic Hybrids gleam in reflected sunlight, and are set off perfectly by their huge rust-coloured stamens.

daybreak moves towards dusk. White flowers, so abundant in shape and form, texture and hue, sprinkled delicately or placed with a strong hand, will allow you to create an atmosphere of magic and delight, with plants which will fascinate and reward the enquiring eye. A full appreciation and understanding of white flowers requires a close examination. A casual glance would have you think that white is white and that there is no more to it, but petals vary in hue from pure ice white right through to deep, rich cream, taking in hints of pink and blue, yellow and green on the way. These differing shades combine to create

Introduction

Peonies grow in such a wealth of wonderful forms and colour combinations that it is difficult to choose just a few. One essential for the shopping list is *Paeonia suffruticosa* 'Rock's Variety' with huge crumpled white petals and rich red staining set off by a mass of yellow stamens.

Texture and form have always been my first consideration when selecting plants for a garden design. I would far rather create interesting combinations of foliage shapes, using subtle contrasts of greens, yellows and greys varying in appearance from hard and shiny to soft and furry, than fill a flowerbed with a mass of competing coloured blooms. Indeed it is within such a lush, green setting that white flowers can best display their purity of form and light-reflecting qualities.

The frequently held notion that white flowers are merely 'smart', or indeed 'fashionable', entirely ignores their intense and enduring beauty and astonishing variety of form. In fact, there are white species to be found in every type of plant, whether it be a hardy shrub or a tender alpine. Petals may be thick and waxy or as fragile as tissue paper, they may be splashed with red like spilled ink,

stained with yellow blotches or open up from deep pink buds to reveal a bloom of creamy richness. Close inspection may reveal tiny green spots, delicate blue veining or fluffy orange anthers. Flowers might be huge like trumpets or composed of masses of tiny blooms like a sea of froth.

Whilst working on this book, I have become increasingly impressed by the magical qualities of white flowers and their ability to create a unique mood and atmosphere and now find my original love of these plants nearing obsession in examination of their complex variations. As I live in the centre of London, I especially appreciate their ability to transform a garden into a tranquil retreat from the busy world outside the walls.

Gertrude Jekyll was perhaps first to popularize the idea of planting schemes based on a single colour theme. Her training as a painter combined with a deep love of gardening and detailed knowledge of plant varieties enabled her to create gardens of great subtlety and charm, and her collaboration with the architect Edwin Lutyens resulted in houses and gardens which were considered, in Edwardian England, to be the ultimate in sophistication. Though many of these wonderful houses survive, the majority of their gardens have regrettably been allowed to decline, and evidence of Jekyll's creativity is mainly confined to documentary illustrations. However, one excellent example has been lovingly restored at Barrington Court in Somerset. Even more gratifying for my purposes, it contains an all-white garden which should be visited when at its most glorious, in mid-summer.

Decline and oblivion has certainly not been the fate of the famous gardens at Sissinghurst Castle in Kent. Conceived by Vita Sackville-West, they are now meticulously maintained by the National Trust. Amongst all the beautiful single-colour schemes to be found there, the exquisite white garden, so subtle and tranquil, enclosed within high boundaries has become legendary among garden lovers all over the world. Major Lawrence Johnston, another passionate plantsman of the early part of the twentieth century, devised the majestic landscape at Hidcote in Gloucester-

shire. He also worked on a principle of 'garden rooms', one of which elegantly combines exquisite topiary work with white flowers.

It is my hope that by visiting such gardens and after reading this book, you may be captivated by the possibilities of white gardening and subsequently inspired to devise your own personal interpretation. There certainly is something temptingly quixotic about the idea of an all-white garden, which perhaps draws on a sub-conscious desire for the ultimate in green-fingered purity. Far from being an unattainable luxury, my aim here has been to make the concept of a white garden a practical reality.

Whether your garden can be measured in acres or in yards, I hope that you will take up the challenge to regard your flowers in an entirely new light and go on to create an exciting new dimension in your garden.

Above
The white garden at Barrington Court in Somerset, originally designed by Gertrude Jekyll, is now lovingly maintained to show its original splendour. It is at its best in summer when flowerbeds overflow with frothy petunias and scented tobaccos.

Above left
The charm and variety of white flowers never ceases to surprise. This diminuitive *Gladiolus* species shines like bright stars.

single blooms of the gorgeous, *Eucryphia glutinosa* with its feathery centre. The tender gum tree, *Eucalyptus calophylla* 'Marri', produces spectacular powderpuffs of flowers formed entirely of pale yellow stamens. The yellow markings are so vivid in *Limnanthes douglasii* that it has earned the name of poached egg flower; a stunning annual for the rock garden or border edging. Yellow plays an important role in white lilies such as *L. regale* where it colours the whole centre of the flower and *L. auratum* with a strong yellow stripe accompanied by dark orange speckles resembling splashed paint.

At the cool end of the spectrum are flowers whose inclusion in a white plant list is debatable. However, they make a very valuable 'no-colour' contribution in a white garden adding texture and interest and a good foil for the greens of the foliage. Tremendously prized for winter flowers are the hellebores, of which the most famous must be the white flowering Christmas rose, *Helleborus niger*. However, *H. argutifolius* presents a tight clump of greyish leaves with a dense spike of greenish cup-shaped flowers making it a very elegant evergreen for a grey scheme.

In summer, two annuals offer an extremity of greenness. The tall spikes of *Moluccella laevis*, bells of Ireland, carry minute scented white flowers surrounded by a large green calyx and are excellent for both fresh and dried flower arrangements. In a shady position, the dwarf bedding variety of the tobacco, *Nicotiana affinis* 'Lime Green', offers scented tubular flowers with a startling fluorescent glow.

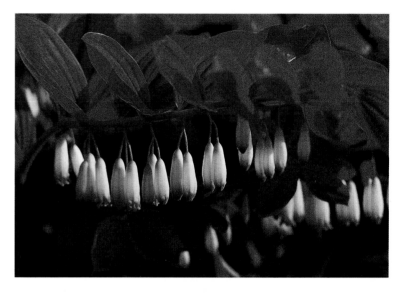

Too good to be kept for the kitchen garden, tall growing angelica makes huge heads of lime green flowers on 1.2 m (4 ft) high stalks above large, heavily incised leaves. Equally architectural, *Euphorbia wulfenii* tops high stems of narrow greyish leaves with dramatic panicles of little lime green bells. Many other members of this strange family also produce

Greenish blooms make a cool and sophisticated statement in an all-white design. For a moist and slightly shady spot *Polygonatum odoratum* (*above*), or *Hydrangea arborescens* 'Grandiflora' (*left*) could be used.

Opposite
Though these flowers have only a very short season in early summer, the architectural foliage of *Paeonia suffruticosa* 'Godaishu' will enhance a white planting scheme.

A Whiter View

Opposite above

A strong supporting background of green trees and shrubs gives body and scale to this sumptuous border. A wide range of flowering plants differing in form, texture and height with shades including pure whites, creams and flesh tones are combined with grey and citrus green foliage. Planted in bold clumps to appear mature and established, they spill over the path softening the edge line.

Opposite below

Foliage plays an important role in the garden particularly when required to provide a setting for white flowers. This border is composed almost entirely of grey toned subjects with a strong accent of fresh new leaves on trees positioned in front of the dark yew hedge. Cream-edged hostas such as, *H. crispula* and *H.* 'Thomas Hogg' accentuate the delicate white blooms around them.

fascinating sulphurous yellow or green flowers.

Many white flowers make the additional contribution of delightful fragrance, bringing yet another dimension to the planting scheme. They should be positioned near the house or along paths to gain the most benefit. Scents of honeysuckle and summer jasmine will drift deliciously through an open window while an arbour of climbing Mme Alfred Carrière roses would complete a romantic hideaway. The perfumed flowers of philadelphus and choisya are both reminiscent of orange blossom, while all the citrus varieties, including lemons and limes, provide masses of tiny, freshly scented white blooms before their fruits form. Tall growing tobaccos come into their own with both flower and fragrance in the early evening with night scented stocks, insignificant in appearance, but astonishingly perfumed at the end of the day.

Some flowers have rich and cloying perfumes and may be grown in pots to be enjoyed in the house or conservatory. For example, lilies, gardenias and stephanotis all give a profusion of exotically scented bloom over a long period of time. More delicately, shallow pots filled with paper-white narcissi or miniature cyclamen would be delightful for winter scent indoors.

Foliage Framework

Pale and beautiful as they are, white flowers will not stand alone. Strong sunshine can appear to diminish delicate blooms which may lose their definition leaving only an impression of the larger, more dominant

flowers. To be shown to best advantage they need to be given a backdrop and supporting cast. Foliage with all its diversity of colour, form and texture fulfils these roles and will also provide an extra dimension of its own.

The careful selection and placing of foliage plants will bring scale and balance to your design. Evergreens in particular are invaluable for permanent effect. They provide a framework for the overflowing plants and a darker background to set off pale flowers. Particularly dramatic results can be obtained with evergreens using strong contrasts of line and bold geometric shapes to create a planting picture which will continue right through the winter.

However, the desired effect in many cases does not want to be too heavy; the contrast between very dark green leaves and white flowers can appear too strong, resulting in an artificial and staged effect. The gentler greens of deciduous shrubs and herbaceous perennials generally give a soft and subtle framework, not in competition with the flowers but providing green spaces from which they can emerge. These lush plants create a gentle atmosphere with their newly formed fresh spring foliage in shades of pinky bronze and brilliant greens, making a wonderful foil for early bulbs and delicate spring flowers. Ferns and poolside plants grow up quickly in spring rains too, transforming the look of the garden in a matter of days.

Herbaceous plants which die down in winter must grow very fast to attain their ultimate heights of anything up to 2.4 m (8 ft) in one season. Care must be taken when siting these giants, that they do not leave too great

16

an area completely bare in the dormant months. Judicious underplanting, however, and the artful placing of evergreen subjects will help to fill the gaps with interest.

Tall growing bamboo makes a perfect contrast to broader leaved plants such as gunnera, hosta and lysichiton, its clear elegant lines being made of graceful stems covered in slim, short leaves, combining to make a consistently atmospheric rustling movement. Grasses, too, give a fine etched effect with narrow leaves of blue-green tones, or green striped with yellow or white. Their height varies from 10 cm to 2.4 m (4 in to 8 ft) tall, with leaves in curved masses below high flower plumes or branching angularly along the length of tall stems. Among the other plants, their foliage gives a uniquely soft texture, never competing with the white blossoms around them.

Grey leaved plants have a sun bleached look about them which can be used to create a Mediterranean air in colder climates, though they must be planted in a sunny site. They combine particularly well with white flowers which shine amongst them with silvery and luminous effect.

The size of plant and choice of leaf shape will be determined by the scale of your overall design and qualities of the flowers you choose. An eye for contrast and subtle differences in colour and texture is needed and care must be taken to prevent dominant plants overwhelming the scheme. Bold leaves need boldly shaped flowers to stand up to them; alternatively, a group of smaller plants clumped together will provide a sufficiently strong effect.

Opposite
Town gardens are often small and enclosed by high walls. Although these serve an essential function providing much needed privacy, they also create shady spots where flowers are reluctant to perform. The boundary fences of this intimate terrace have been smothered with layer upon layer of evergreen ivy, laurel, holly and mahonia to make a permanent year-round screen, while helxine and tiny herbs look charming growing amongst the paving stones. Although white flowers have been confined almost to two pots of marguerites framing the seat, much use could be made of summer annuals such as busy Lizzie and tobacco, both of which flourish in the shade. Spring bulbs including tulips, crocus and narcissus are invaluable too, for an early show of bloom.

Taller varieties would normally be placed at the back of the border, allowing more delicate plants to be seen to best advantage, though a bold statement set in the middle of lower growing plants can often look stunningly effective. Broad or stubby leaves may be contrasted with the vertical lines of slender flower spikes or narrow leaves; a filigree of lacy leaves works well against smoother shapes, and patterned leaves with plain. Amongst these differing shapes of leaves the forms of flowers must be considered in the same way; each plant complementing its neighbours, whether in a mass of large or blowzy flowers or a delicate froth of tiny ones. They will vary from cream to white to pale green, among the leaves. Dark foliage next to light, blue hosta with green fern, silver artemisia with purple sage.

Evergreen

The strongest element amongst all the plants is that of the evergreen shrubs and trees, whose permanent leaf colour and bold forms provides the framework for the garden design. Whether employed as hedging, perhaps in the formal shapes of topiary, or as key shrubs placed strategically to give emphasis or structure for the border, they are the bones around which to build your garden. Evergreen hedges can provide a solid background or act as a windbreak while woodland rhododendrons will create a tall but gentler looking screen.

Evergreens have a denser, more permanent quality than the fleeting foliage of deciduous trees, whose leaves are fragile and translucent in spring, ageing to gold and red in autumn. In spite of their dark colour, evergreens include some of the most glamorous flowering plants there are; camellias, *Magnolia grandiflora*, rhododendrons and azaleas, scented *Choisya ternata*, eucryphia, yucca, eucalyptus and many more. Add to the list the fruit bearing evergreens and consider how many species flower in winter, and you will see how indispensable their contribution is. In addition, many conifers offer cones and fruit and grow in a variety of clean shapes like ready-made topiary, offering a whole host of possibilities. Evergreen species are essential for the creation of topiary shapes, whether of box, bay or yew and, used as low hedging, can turn a garden into pure geometry, a veritable chess-board of planting spaces.

Fatsia japonica, with leaves like giant hands and a haze of pale branched flower heads in the autumn, grows huge in the shade and provides wonderful atmosphere in a cool dark corner. With glaucous blue hosta, mottled lamium and a collection of ferns, a leafy grotto might take shape, mysterious in the shadows; a place where lily of the valley and anemones will naturalize, peeping out in spring, while helxine and pearlwort creep between damp stones.

A secret glade of rhododendrons with clusters of huge white flowers almost hiding the leaves might lead through clumps of gentle foxgloves with tall spires of flowers of speckled cream or white, and frothy meadow sweet, both welcoming the resulting dappled light. On venturing further, an arbour, for romance and secret assignations, might be surrounded by camellias whose dark, glossy

Above
A dark yew hedge provides an ideal backdrop for white flowers allowing their shape and texture to show through. Here, tall spikes of delphinium contrast well with graceful arching spiraea and a huge flowered climbing clematis.

Above right
The searing blue and spikey form of the clump-forming grass *Festuca glauca* makes an elegant and unexpected partner to the tall growing *Anemone japonica* and soft white roses beyond, against the dark foliage framework.

appearance is transformed with a fabulous display of white flowers of unimaginable beauty so early in the year. Or a pergola dripping with long racemes of white wisteria followed in summer by sprays of creamy roses, their delicious scent filling the air, accompanied by drifts of exotic perfumed lilies and tobaccos.

A paved courtyard, normally looking at its best in spring and summer with pots and troughs filled with ever changing bedding plants, can be given a year round treatment by using some permanent evergreen varieties such as euonymus and ivies amongst the white flowers. Some containers should be planted with single specimens such as mop-head bay trees or spiky dracaenas to make permanent architectural statements of formal symmetry amongst them. Behind, *Magnolia grandiflora* would clothe a wall with magnificent dark leaves, unfurling its enormous butter coloured flowers scented with a heady mix of lemon and spice.

Grey and Silver

One of the most natural associations in the all-white garden is that of silver and grey foliage. There is a really wide choice of material, ranging from the tall and dramatic to the creeping and diminutive, even allowing an entire planting scheme to be created without the use of any flowers at all, if so desired. The qualities of grey and silver foliage are quite unique with their cooling effect on a summer's day or quietly glowing at dusk. All together, they have an invaluable role to play in the creation of a white garden.

Many silver and grey subjects are tough skinned creatures, used to being baked by the sun, so lend themselves to an open, well-drained site, their roots unable to tolerate long periods of wet and cold. If you have a site with poor soil, masses of sun and a shortage of water, in other words, quite impossible for most types of cultivation, these plants will come to your rescue. South and west facing walls will not only shelter them from freezing winter winds, but conserve the heat of the sun long after it has gone down to provide a warm microclimate; all do well next to paving which absorbs and reflects the sun's warmth. Many

Empty spaces often exist in a newly planted border or occur because of seasonal changes. By moving an established pot of silvery *Centaurea gymnocarpa* from the terrace an instant architectural statement has been created in the middle of an otherwise undistinguished bed.

grey plants are suitable for seaside locations, tough enough to withstand their salt laden and drying winds which cause gardeners such headaches.

Their leaves, adapted to conserve moisture, are sometimes almost metallic in their sheen, sometimes woolly and thick, sometimes like felt or suede. Their curiously tactile qualities are even more appealing. Some combine appearance with the powerful fragrance of aromatic oils, making a sunny afternoon in the garden a heady mixture of sensations. So why not use an otherwise unpromising location with hot, dry conditions to your advantage and create a sculptural display rich in smells, textures and leaf shapes?

The fact that most flowers of silver leaved plants are not white should not deter you from using them, except perhaps in the most strict planting specifications. Many are bluish, like lavender, or soft and inoffensive silvery pinks, which blend in subtly. Of course, many are searingly bright yellows, like senecio, but the flowering season is quite short so why not just snip them off? It would be a pity to cut the sulphur yellow blooms from *Verbascum olympicum* though. From a clump of huge velvety leaves at the base of the plant, emerge several 1.5 m (5 ft) spires surmounted by these eye-catching flowers.

Silvers and greys are good mixers when handled sensitively, looking best with glaucous

blue or soft purple foliage and the darker blue greens. They can also make sensational architectural specimens. One of the best candidates for this purpose is the cardoon, *Cynara cardunculus*, with its huge, boldly cut silver grey leaves from which shoot long thick stems with enormous thistle-shaped heads. Cut and dried, these make magnificent winter decorations. Also standing to 2 m (7 ft) is *Macleaya cordata*. This spreads quickly providing a dense thicket of large, deeply indented grey leaves which hold clusters of sparkling water droplets after rain.

Delicate variation of form can be achieved by the use of slender grasses of which there are some stunning blue–grey varieties perfect for hot, dry sites. *Festuca glauca* 'Silver Sea' is almost powder blue while *F. punctoria* is steely, sharp and spiky. Similar but denser, is *Koeleria cristata* 'Glauca' which carries matching blue-grey flower heads. These can all be used as underplanting or massed together in clumps to form a sculptural feature.

Evergreen herbs such as rosemary, sage and rue also relish sunny, dry conditions and the understated blue and purple tones in their leaves add depth to the silver and grey. For edges and low hedging, in a topiary garden for example, try the white flowering lavender, *L. angustifolia* 'Nana Alba' which grows to 30 cm (12 in) high. *Santolina chamaecyparissus corsica* makes a tiny whitish grey bush, very suitable for edging, as is the strongly aromatic silver thyme with attractive variegated foliage. For a taller result, use *S. chamaecyparissus* with its silver feathered leaves. *Hebe* 'Pagei', though tender in colder areas, can be introduced as an alternative variety of low edging;

it makes a dense mound of tiny greyish glaucous leaves with pretty white flowers in late summer.

With clever use of sun lovers, a south facing courtyard can be given all the atmosphere of the Mediterranean. A raised patio, grouped with tubs of white oleander and plumbago and bush or standard marguerites, could have steps edged with pots of pelargoniums and petunias leading down to the main beds which might be arranged around a circular path. A mass of yuccas planted together, their strong, spiky shapes and dramatic spires of white flowers rising high above, could then combine to make the central feature of the garden. White lavender, cistus, dianthus and marguerites sited amongst strong statements of silvery leaves would fill the beds, backed for contrast, by tall clumps of *Phormium tenax* with its variegated blue–green or bronze spear-shaped leaves.

Window boxes and hanging baskets filled with honey scented alyssum and zonal pelargoniums with white *Campanula isophylla* to spill over the edges would be given a more ethereal appearance with the addition of grey and silver trailing nepeta and *Helichrysum petiolaris* with feathery *Cineraria maritima* for height. The ivy-leaved pelargonium, 'Elegance' with its glaucous, grey-green leaves edged in white, and soft, pinkish white flowers, also trails prettily, or, for contrast, some of the scented pelargoniums have pungently aromatic grey foliage.

A gentle bedding theme might use white flowers shining among the gleaming feathery *Artemisia absinthium* 'Lambrook Silver', along with the delightful silken sheen of *Convolvulus cneorum*, its shimmering flowers opening from long, furled pink buds. The intricate blue filigree of rue leaves and the pale narrow foliage of dianthus would complement glaring rock roses and dimorphotheca, while furry, everlasting anaphalis and self-seeded Iceland poppies would meander unhindered amongst them. Spires, of *Campanula pyramidalis* 'Alba' and eremurus would punctuate the design, with soft bushes of old ivory roses and white musk mallow massed around to link them all together. Arching stems of white flowered buddleia covered in butterflies are all that is needed to complete this charming scene.

Variegated Leaves

Plain green leaves, whether evergreen or deciduous, are not the only effective form of foliage, of course. Patterned foliage will soften the outlines of a garden, lightening the effect and, by providing contrast, will enhance the other greens. Used cleverly, brightly variegated leaves can be as striking as the white flowers themselves.

White-edged leaves can create a rather delicate and lacy effect making a somewhat feminine planting scheme, while by contrast, larger leaves, perhaps with strong gold or yellow stripes, can act as a dramatic foil to create an impression of strength and simplicity.

Evergreen shrubs in plain colours have their part to play, but they can look very heavy and dominating. However, great interest and relief can be provided by variegated forms such as holly; *Ilex* × *altaclerensis* 'Golden King'

Opposite
The role of grey and silver foliage in the white garden is quite unique for its properties of texture and tone. Leaves may be smooth and gleaming or heavily coated in fur or down such as those of *Verbascum olympicum*. This giant makes a superbly dramatic statement best seen planted on its own and allowed to develop into a huge clump as it has done here. Purists might want to cut off the sulphurous yellow flowers as they develop on the branching spikes.

and 'Silver Queen' positively sparkle in winter frost, and the soft pink new growth which appears in spring is quite delightful. This variety is so lively in comparison to the usual dark green and can be trained to a formal mop-head shape to make an interesting feature planted in a tub near the house, especially at Christmas time.

Variegated ivies exist in innumerable varieties and leaf shapes. As ground cover, trailing from a window box or climbing up a wall, they give an entirely brighter image than their dark green cousin *Hedera helix*, glowering in shady places where paler forms would be unable to grow. *Euonymus japonicus* and the smaller *E. fortunei* have smooth oval leaves and each has contrasting variegated forms in white. *E. fortunei* also has a gold variegated form. They are very different in effect and could even be planted together to set each other off. For winter colour, *Eleagnus × ebbingei* 'Limelight' has soft yellow leaves edged and marked with green and backed with bright silver creating a dense but luminous effect; a real delight on gloomy days.

In a sunny sheltered space, myrtle can charm in all its different forms but the variegated *Myrtus communis* is particularly pretty. Its single white five petalled flowers are almost hidden beneath enormous tufts of stamens; scattered among soft green glossy leaves with white edges, they give a jewelled effect against dark green or grey foliage.

For cover, variegated periwinkle, *Vinca minor* 'Variegata' is a bright, clear cream with green markings and *Pachysandra terminalis* is soft green with pale edging and white tubular flowers at the end of each stem. Both these plants are good with spring bulbs growing through them with larger flowering shrubs behind; they are useful too, filling spaces left by such foliage perennials as hostas when they die back in the winter.

There are variegated forms of many more evergreens, including the conifers, but herbaceous and deciduous plants with fresh new leaves appearing each spring, give subtler effects and broaden the range of colour, to include bronze, grey-greens and lime yellows. Even small bulbs can play their part; *Erythronium* 'White Pagoda', the dog's-tooth violet has leaves mottled in shades of green and brown, while the diversity of silvery green patterned foliage found in the tiny woodland cyclamen is every bit as attractive as the delicate flowers. Planted beneath a silver birch they will reflect the shimmering bark, flowering in autumn and spring while the tree is bare of leaves. *Arum italicum* 'Pictum' has pale markings on arrow-shaped leaves appearing late in the year while other perennials are still underground.

Hostas are unsurpassed for their sculptural forms and the beauty of their glaucous foliage. They produce huge clumps of spear-shaped leaves in sophisticated shades of grey-blue and lime green and in subtle combinations of stripes and edging. *Hosta fortunei* 'Albopicta' is deep green with a broad yellow splash in the centre of each leaf and *H. f.* 'Aureomarginata' reverses the theme with a strong golden outline.

A combination of early bulbs and rich hostas could be joined by the white flowering lungwort, 'Sissinghurst White' with its spectacularly mottled foliage, with *Anemone nemo-*

rosa, oxalis and white scilla; taller growing mottled foxgloves would complete this charming woodland scene.

Grasses planted in soft clumps look even more effective in their variegated forms; *Glyceria maxima* 'Variegata' with its white and yellow striped leaves does very well near water, or for an open site, the invasive ribbon grass, *Phalaris arundinacea* 'Picta' has white edged, grey leaves.

Deciduous shrubs and trees have a vital part to play in the texture of the garden, with variegated leaf forms giving them a light and often frothy appearance, less overwhelming than the evergreens. The dogwood, *Cornus alba* 'Elegantissima' and *Weigela florida* 'Variegata' both have delicate looking leaves with creamy margins. Taller growing, *Aralia elata* 'Variegata' produces large white and green leaves to create an overall shimmering effect. Dramatic wedding cake layers of white and green foliage decorate the unusual *Cornus controversa* 'Variegata' making it a fine specimen in a shrub border.

Left
Variegated foliage can create a white effect of its own. *Aralia elata* 'Variegata' makes a gentle looking shrub, softened further by its frothy cream flower panicles, pinkish stems and young leaves.

Opposite
Contrasts in form as well as colour add depth and scale. Here, variegated foliage is divided between a massed effect of small ovate leaves of *Weigela florida* 'Variegata' and strong clumps of blade-like variegated iris which give accent below.

Where
White is Right

The Planning Stage

White flowers, with their cool, elegant and somewhat fragile aesthetic qualities, need a sensitive hand and eye to compose a fitting setting for them. They are seldom brash or showy, rather more a delicate palette of subtle tints and forms. On the whole they appear much more at home nestling amongst a supportive framework of foliage to give contrast to their paleness. In scorching sun they appear to shrivel in front of your eyes looking limp and unhappy on an exposed site; they prefer to be sheltered by a background of mellow walls or tall hedges. Given the right environment, they glow on grey days whilst other flowers look gloomy; on sunlit days they shine, performing with pride to offer warmth and gaiety.

It is important to provide a suitable site for a white garden, more from the point of view of background or isolation from competing flowers than from the soil type or geographical location. A tremendous range of white flowering varieties exists amongst all plant types, from trees and shrubs to herbaceous perennials, annuals and bulbs. Whether your soil is acid or alkaline, moist or dry, an exciting planting scheme can be devised.

The white garden's scope will be determined, to a large extent, by the overall size of your garden, and then by the amount of space within your garden which you wish to give over to it. A disproportionately large area devoted to a white garden might present accordingly great planning difficulties; it might lose its aesthetic value, being out of balance with its surroundings, and spreading a good thing too far and too thin. You might then be well advised to consider a smaller plot

which could be enclosed by walls, fencing or hedges; in this way the white effect will be concentrated and defined to make a much stronger visual statement.

A large garden may provide a choice of suitable locations, but bearing in mind the need to create an enclosure, it would make economic and planning sense to select an existing boundary for a starting point. From this, plan a square or rectangular plot in proportion to the rest of the garden, and of a size that will be convenient to manage. A typical long, narrow town garden presents itself as a perfect candidate for division and enclosure; having two long boundaries, a short rear one, and the house on the fourth side, it may be divided roughly into three equal rectangles. The open sides of the rectangle could then be bordered by fences or walls. A path from the house (not necessarily running symmetrically through the middle) would lead to a door or gate into the white garden, and passing through it, would then lead out to yet another garden beyond.

Walled gardens have deliciously romantic

Above
Twin borders of delicate white *Malva moschata alba* are disected here by a green walkway of sweelty-scented camomile. A brick edging serves to define and crispen the effect, while the whole scene is framed by topiary hedges and tall beech trees.

Above right
Clear white tulips combine crisply with low clumps of silvery-grey foliage of *Pyrus salicifolia* in this fresh spring garden. The huge round box tree with its young green foliage effectively separates this scene from the rest of the garden.

Just one variety of pure white roses is planted along this wall and shows just how effective a single strong statement can be. These deliciously scented and wonderfully romantic old-fashioned varieties offer a charm with which no modern forms can compare.

Left
Walled gardens offer the possibility of a romantic hideaway and this one has all the right ingredients. Dense foliage overflows the boundaries while a rose covered archway allows access to this secret retreat. A pair of white painted benches flanked formally by a row of four urns are all that is needed to bring the garden to life.

connotations and offer privacy and a retreat from the outside world. They also present scope for a multitude of briefs, horticulturally speaking. Large country houses always created walled kitchen gardens where the shelter afforded from chilling winds and the warmth absorbing qualities of bricks would be well appreciated. The microclimate created by these walls makes it possible to grow many tender shrubs and herbs which would otherwise be destined for warmer climes. Fruit trees, too, will benefit if trained, espalier fashion, against a warm wall. They will ripen earlier and crop more heavily.

Visually, walls add a vertical dimension to the planting plan, allowing a multitude of beautiful climbers and vines to be grown. A selection of glorious wisteria, perfumed jasmine, clematis and sumptuous roses are a must for any white garden, and dark and mellow brickwork makes a perfect background for their pale blooms. Walled gardens do not impose any restrictions on the planting style within, formal or relaxed treatments being equally at home. The principal decision at this stage, however, concerns the design and choice of construction materials; these must primarily match those of adjoining buildings as closely as possible, and in design they must be sympathetic with the environment, not compete with it. Rendered blockwork makes a good and economic substitute for bricks where these are not available or appropriate.

In situations where timber is a more natural choice, there are many types of fencing which may be used to form an enclosure. Rustic poles arranged as a dense screen would blend

Below left
The immaculate topiary work in the white garden at Hidcote has taken many decades to mature but inspiration can be taken from it for a more instant scheme. For example, ready grown bird and animals figures of buxus are available and an enclosing hedge can be created from the fast growing Lawson's cypress, instead of the more traditional yew.

Far right
In a relatively small town garden it may be desirable to devote the entire space to white flowers. The north American dogwoods produce pure white single blooms in spring and look quite stunning here against a background of richly-coloured brickwork. Alpines such as saxifrage, arabis and iberis would all be suitable for border edging to foil the formal herringbone paving design.

naturally into a wooded landscape. A more elaborate timber structure might reflect the architecture of a contemporary house, perhaps coloured with paint to set off the white flower design. A deep blue-green can look amazingly good as an unexpected foil for greys and yellow-green foliage. In a hot, sunny location, topaz blue or even vibrant pink could give a unique and exotic angle to a white planting theme, reversing the norm of a white background with coloured flowers.

The art of topiary, practised and perfected from the seventeenth to the nineteenth century is currently enjoying a resurgence of interest. Images of intricate Elizabethan knot gardens fronting a Jacobean façade readily come to mind, as do fantastical railway engines in front gardens, or peacocks and teddy bears planted in lawns. These ambitious projects, created with slow growing, small-leaved evergreen box or yew, have taken decades or even centuries to mature. Today's social climate with its need for instant effect and a tendency to move home every few years demands different criteria for the creation of a topiary scheme.

Container-grown plants, though fairly ex-

pensive, provide the solution as hedges can be established very quickly by using mature material. A controlled and formal framework of low hedges made from green box or grey foliage plants, such as santolina or white lavender, would make a suitably elegant setting. The beds or compartments thus formed might each display a different white flower creating a delightful growing tapestry. Such a scheme need not be for the pleasure of a large country estate alone; it would adapt itself perfectly to a formal town situation, complementing a classical façade with charm and elegance.

In a town garden, white flowers have a really significant role to play. These spaces, often shaded by tall buildings or overgrown street trees planted with such good intentions many decades ago, can be very short on sunshine. Owners are often away all day and see their gardens mainly in evening light, and the faintly luminescent qualities of white flowers are really to be appreciated in these shadowy conditions. White flowers near the house can be enjoyed right through the hours of darkness, as they reflect some of the light spilling from the windows, or they may be

and cover the ground. Hang wire baskets from the wall, plant flowering shrubs like hydrangeas or camellias in large tubs, grow climbing *Clematis montana* 'Alba' up balustrading or trellis and fill pots and baskets with cheerful annuals like pelargoniums and petunias. If you want to keep white-painted walls for maximum reflection of light, grow some ivy and Virginia creeper over them in places, to provide contrast for the white flowers. Otherwise, a pale terracotta would give an interesting yet unobtrusive background, particularly lovely if natural terracotta pots are used. The overall effect here would be sophisticated but at the same time comfortable and soft.

Town spaces need all the help they can get from softening plants. If the street side of the house is treated as unstintingly as its more private rear, the environment benefits incalculably. So do not be selfish; think of the joy and inspiration you can bring to passers-by and visitors if you fill your window sills with overflowing boxes of flowers and baskets hanging over the porch. If you have steps, line them with a blooming procession of plant pots. Sadly, in some areas, you may have to cement them to the ground, but the trouble is surely worthwhile.

Country dwellers with extensive gardens to organize are sometimes amazed at the achievements of their urban cousins. It often seems that given restrictions or limitations we perform much more creatively than we would with an enormous blank canvas at our disposal. However, one of the great pleasures of wandering through the gardens of a large country house is arriving at the herbaceous

picked out by lights installed in the garden. It would be quite valid to consider a totally white small town garden, where other colours would not give such an all-round performance.

A delightful summer outdoor eating area close to the house could be achieved by setting it entirely amongst night scented tobaccos and luminous impatiens, perhaps with sweetly perfumed jasmine and honeysuckle trained up and over a pergola to give privacy. Petals would glow in the flickering candlelight, with perfume pervading the still evening air to grace a perfect, romantic assignation.

A small city plot may only run to a tiny front entrance area with steps down into a light-well. Even with such restrictions a white garden is possible; be uninhibited here and aim for maximum impact; cram in as many plant pots as possible. All sizes will have a place; run them down the edges of the steps

Bold and generous planting statements are always desirable where space permits. The rear of a herbaceous border is enhanced by the massive incised grey foliage of the ornamental cardoon. This sun-baked situation, with its inviting white bench, is a perfect spot to grow the perennial daisy *Osteospermum* 'La Mortola', which is covered in gleaming white blooms with mauve undersides throughout the summer.

border. Here, in its great and abundant glory, can be seen all the most desirable of garden flowering perennials. Astonishingly tall spikes of foxtail lily, with plumes of tiny flowers 2.4 m (8 ft) high, all but steal the show from equally stately spires of giant delphinium. Cimicifuga and lysimachia, though less familiar, also give a spiky show. Clouds of little white flowers float above the cabbage-leaved crambe, and the equally ephemeral gypsophila also gives light relief. Everlasting anaphalis, late flowering Japanese anemones, glorious madonna lilies, luscious peonies and exuberant oriental poppies all have their place here.

There have to be disadvantages, however, in all areas of life. Herbaceous borders do require endless amounts of staking, deadheading, cutting down and clearing away, not to mention feeding, mulching and dividing for replanting. They are not a pretty sight in winter, dried and browning leaves alone remaining where glorious blooms once reigned. Today, when help is seldom available and time, let alone space, is at a premium, a much more successful solution may be de-

rived from combining these lovely perennials with hard-working and good value flowering shrubs.

Chosen from both evergreen and deciduous species, these will give a framework and structure to the border. They do not die down or require eternal maintenance. All that is basically required is a little pruning after flowering to keep them in good shape, and the removal of dead or weak wood. There are white flowering shrubs to suit all climates and soils, and varieties which give a show in all months of the year. With careful strategy and planning it is possible to create a mixed border to satisfy and delight the most exacting plantsperson. A simple background to give shelter and contrast would be desirable; if no existing wall or fence is available, a fast-growing evergreen hedge of Lawson's cypress could be established quite quickly.

Such a mixed border is reasonably easy to place. A fairly open site with average to good soil is all that is required, though planting beds should be well prepared in advance by incorporating extra organic material such as peat or compost, and a dressing of bone meal to help roots to establish themselves. Aftercare in the first season is important. Lavish watering followed without delay by a mulch of bark chippings will help preserve moisture and discourage weed seedlings. Frequent, regular waterings must be given throughout the first summer, being especially careful if the weather is dry and planting took place in the spring.

While the desire may exist for such an ambitious scheme, the space in which to carry it out may not. A very pleasing result can be achieved by devoting just one section of the border, or one corner of the garden to white flowers. This could be separated aesthetically but not physically from its neighbours by groups of grey foliage varieties, thus creating contrast and a further visual dimension.

White Style

All the great gardens of the world, those which make a profound impression on us and stay in our memories, have one significant thing in common: style. Visual statements are being made; sometimes within a strong architectural framework with imposing schemes to complement an impressive estate, such as Lord Aberconway's at Bodnant in Wales. Here dignified Italianate terraces are framed by equally stately topiaries of yew, walls are clothed in Japanese wisteria, and magnolias reach staggering proportions.

The concept of terraced gardens was taken to even more aspiring heights on the steep shores of Lake Como in northern Italy. Here steps and statuary lead the visitor up and up, through a succession of formal gardens of what is now somewhat faded magnificence. Neighbouring Lake Maggiore boasts the astonishing Isola Bella, a unique and gracious island garden with nine stepped terraces, colonnades and a 'water theatre', built in the seventeenth century for the Borromeo family. More recently, the contemporary Brazilian garden architect, Burle Marx, has created dramatic landscapes of native cacti and tropical plants to suit such visionary planning schemes as the futuristic city of Brasilia. In Barcelona, the organically inspired Parque

Güell by Antoni Gaudi employed spiky, indigenous palms and yuccas to emphasize elaborate mosaic terraces and colonnaded walkways.

All these parks and gardens have been devised by people for whom design is a fundamental element of life, who have vision and the opportunity both to challenge accepted ideas and to change the landscape. However, some of the most charming gardens are built on a more intimate scale; these are created by their owners, people passionate about plants, who lived and worked closely with them. Vita Sackville-West worked like this at Sissinghurst, Major Lawrence

Above left
Two huge clumps of the daisy-flowered *Chrysanthemum maximum* frame the entrance to this timber cottage.

Above right
Formal planting designs do not necessarily result in rigid effects. The sequential siting of huge buddleia bushes is foiled by their loose habit, while the stone urns are almost obscured by tumbling masses of petunias and marguerites.

Left
This courtyard provides a springtime retreat, surrounded by high topiary hedges of yew and planted with *Narcissus* 'Thalia'.

33

Johnston at Hidcote and the painter, Monet, at Giverny in northern France.

Monet's garden at Giverny is informed by the same artistic vision as his impressionist paintings. Structure is at once developed, defined, and diffused by soft drifts of colour. An artist's palette has been let loose, resulting in a delightfully relaxed and dreamy vista of summer flowers. Both at Hidcote and Sissinghurst, large spaces have been divided formally into smaller garden compartments, each one either representing a different planting theme or dominated by specific colourings. This has resulted in gardens of great style, intimate in scale and closely reflecting the character of their creators.

In order to define what style actually is, it is first necessary to isolate it from taste: they are not the same thing at all. Taste is very subjective and personal: fortunately its varied forms offer a colourful world of multiple images giving us the opportunity to speculate on what is 'good' or what is 'bad'. Though style is personal too, it can be appreciated and admired without actually being liked or desired. Visually it results from the combination of a 'good eye' and the courage to follow one's ideas through without wavering.

Personal style in dressing and decoration will follow through naturally to style in the garden. You will almost certainly find that you will wish to invoke a similar character there to the one which pervades the rest of your life. Creating this style if you are new to gardening may pose a challenge to you but you will soon find that visiting established gardens and searching through books will help to trigger the imagination enormously.

Gardens work visually when they are handled firmly, with attention being paid to form and scale. Surrounding architecture and landscape must be complemented by the planting, either flowing with it or accentuating it. There is no need to be hidebound by aesthetic convention though, for a garden is a personal creation where fantasy should be allowed to reign.

Urban dwellers often dream of moving to 'the country'. This image of peace and tranquillity with space all around and the time to enjoy it is well rooted in many an aspiring gardener's psyche. If your dream is to create a cottage garden even though you live in the middle of town, then there is absolutely no reason why you should not do it; you had better grow roses round the kitchen door to link it to the house, though.

Your romantic plot will be tightly packed with tall growing hollyhocks and lupins, with clematis and old roses smothering rustic arches, all interspersed with annual flowers resulting from an over exuberant hand with the seed packets in spring. Frothy clouds of cosmos will vie with sweet smelling pinks, spires of delphiniums with night scented stocks. It will feel soft and pretty with comfortable old-fashioned values. Please make sure that you have an open, sunny situation for this dream, however, or you will be rewarded only by mildew and frugal blooms.

If you are an adventurous creature and high drama is more your style, then an exotic theme might be the one for you. The word exotic implies tropical climates, dense rain forests inhabited by parrots and epiphytic orchids, giant creepers and fantastic flowers.

It is in fact quite possible to recreate this effect in cooler climates by growing plants with enormous leaves or curious shapes. Even banana plants and tree ferns can be grown in sheltered situations.

Gunnera manicata is a suitably exotic plant which terrifies as many gardeners as it intrigues, and is more reminiscent of strange prehistoric monsters than of gentle flower arrangers in print frocks. Unsurprisingly, it is of Brazilian origin, and is easily the largest-leaved plant you can grow, each leaf unfurling on a spiny stem to a size of 1.8 m (6 ft) in all directions. A rough deeply veined surface adds to the excitement, and the whole plant is set off by an immense flowering stem resembling a giant pine cone. Do not be put off by the fact that the whole plant may cover an area 5.4 m (18 ft) wide; just think how much you will have left in your budget for flowers. White flowers need to be selected with care with such a majestic plant to partner. They must be planted in big groups or else they will simply disappear. Clumps of stately arums, like those seen in primitive Mexican paintings, are a must; as is the aptly named white lily, *Cardiocrinum giganteum*, with its immense spikes of creamy white tubular flowers. Shrubs like white *Hibiscus syriacus* and *Romneya coulteri*, the Californian tree poppy, have suitably exuberant flowers to fit into this picture. You may be a little short on flowering variety in such a scheme, but never on conversation openers.

This kind of exotic jungle setting would be a perfect foil to a modern house, but would be equally at home creating a lush, informal water garden, or to display an imposing

sculpture. It is full of powerful images and vibrant texture: a garden to satisfy the adventurer.

All this talk of drama and profusion may make you long for formality and control. Not for you the Russian vine smothering the potting shed, or jungle triffids invading the lawn. You admire scale but with balance, you love flowers but want to see them alone, in their own space. The measure and control of Bach appeals rather than the extravagant temperament of Berlioz.

A cool, restrained topiary scheme, with planting carefully calculated and everything in its place, might offer just the right stylistic opportunity. It certainly does not have to be based on an Elizabethan knot garden; it could be organized in a less conventional way. Beds could be set on the diagonal, giving a more asymmetrical viewpoint with planting heights varied to balance. Less common but quick to establish border and hedging material such as

A picket fence makes a secure but informal enclosure for the relaxed planting style of a cottage garden. This one provides support for climbing roses and a sympathetic backdrop for a simple flowering border which includes poppies, ox-eye daisies and furry-grey lamb's ears.

silver thyme or white lavender would make a refreshing and sophisticated departure from predictable green box.

An extremely elegant scheme might use only grey foliage subjects to form the borders, including aromatic herbs and shrubs. Seasonal flowers could then be used for bedding, thus offering the opportunity to keep the garden fresh for most of the year. Tulips, daffodils and hyacinth accompanied by pansies during the early months would give way to phlox and verbena, petunia and nicotiana, with cosmos and matricaria taking it right through to the first frosts.

Another cool gardening style comes from Japan. There, designs to honour religious themes sometimes consist primarily of raked gravel, a few carefully placed stones and a symbolic conifer tree. Water plays an important role while thick bamboo poles tied together ingeniously with string tend to be used as fencing. Stylistically pure though this is, we as Westerners, might find such a garden too rigid and unyielding. The main elements can be taken as a foundation, however, for a more fluid and varied arrangement, more pleasing to a non-Oriental eye.

Rustic poles are more easily available than bamboo, and worked vertically, close together, they make a good substitute for the background fence. Growing bamboos, tall and graceful, would then form the predominant foliage framework, unusual conifers being added for texture. By creating stepped levels in the garden, water could then be allowed to flow down into a small pool where goldfish might dawdle. Cobbles and gravel are equally suitable for the paths and the feathery white flowers and ferny foliage of astilbe or aruncus would complement the bamboo beautifully. Dictamnus, epimedium, Solomon's seal and meadow rue also deserve a place. This delicate planting accompanied by the sound of trickling water would create a private and contemplative retreat from the busy world outside.

A passionate plantsperson is probably far less concerned with style than with the challenge and delight of growing as many species and unusual varieties as possible. Interesting as such gardens can be from an academic point of view, sufficient consideration is not always given to form and overall effect. While plants may be growing beautifully, if attention is not given to the balance of heights and forms, textures and tone, then their visual benefits are diminished.

Realizing the potential of the planting material and structuring its layout advantageously achieves white style in this situation. It is all part of those first principles of foliage colour, texture and shape combined with flowering form, effect and timing. Plants must be grouped to form strong shapes with delicate flowers planted in large drifts and tall, dramatic species used as visual punctuation marks. White flowers have inherent style but sensitive aesthetic handling is essential to bring out the best in them. Sensitive does not mean weak though; style requires not only insight but also the courage to make statements. Here the intention is to create a style of some opulence, perhaps even grandeur; this garden should be a generous and overflowing vision, full of interest and diversity to give constant and developing pleasure.

White for All Seasons

Year after year the evolution of the seasons repeats itself in a constant pattern. Cold and moody winter suddenly becomes bright and optimistic spring; summer develops with all its luxury of foliage and flower, then, just as smoothly, autumn takes over with its opulent fruits and rich hues. Each season has its qualities; in each season are to be found favourites and forgotten delights.

Planning a garden which will have interest all the year round is always a challenge; planning an all-white one may be even more of one. There is, however, a more than abundant choice of wonderful subjects from which to choose, for there are white flowers to be found amongst the entire gamut of species with a tremendous variety of habits, styles and tones, and a seasonal range to match.

Opposite above
The deeply incised foliage of *Cynara scolymus* makes a strong architectural feature in a grey planting scheme.

Opposite below
The blue-leaved grass, *Festuca glauca*, creates an unusual textural foil for more familiar grey foliage subjects.

Below
Massive sweeps of naturalized early narcissus make the perfect informal spring planting scheme.

Careful planning is required to keep a white garden in bloom throughout the year. This mixed border is contained by a tall yew hedge, but linked visually to the landscape beyond by a path that leads the eye to an obelisk and a group of tall topiaried trees, which reinforce the design. Dense spikes of *Campanula lactiflora alba* in the foreground also repeat the pyramidal theme and complement the white standard roses, which are also useful for late summer bloom.

If the white garden is to be only one small part of a larger theme it is quite valid to design for one season only; this would really be either spring or summer to benefit from the widest range of subjects and the weather to enjoy them. Because the statement such a garden is making is limited by a finite period of time, it is quite easy to achieve a concentrated effect as space is not wasted by plants waiting to mature in other seasons.

A spring garden would be a perfect device to show off all those gentle woodland flowers and delightful early bulbs. Species tulips like *Tulipa turkestanica*, only 15 cm (6 in) high with a mass of creamy white starlike flowers

on each stem, and the even tinier *Narcissus triandrus* 'Albus', their pale down-turned flowers reminiscent of diminutive curtseying ballerinas, are so special that they deserve a space of their own. A flowering ornamental cherry, like *Prunus* 'Shirotae' makes a delicate backdrop for early woodland flowers. Nestling below you might have nodding dog's-tooth violets with their mottled grey-green leaves, starlike wood anemones or clumps of elegant trilliums. Such a garden can be left to naturalize gently and flower again the following spring with practically no maintenance or attention.

To keep a larger garden furnished with a balance of white flowering plants throughout the year is a supreme challenge, but it is perfectly possible with meticulous planning. The only way to attempt this task is to make a mixed planting scheme which will take advantage of the whole range of shrubs, perennials and annuals available. But do choose carefully; unless your space is endless, plants should be expected to perform generously and must earn their place on the selection list. A flower which only looks perfect for a week may have to be disregarded, however treasured it is.

Shrubs are a fundamental element of year round design. It would even be possible to create a border composed of nothing else as there is such a rich choice of white flowering shrubs with every kind of habit and form. There are deciduous species with rich autumn tints and colourful berries which then proceed to flower on bare winter wood and others whose scented summer flowers are a delight to the senses. Evergreen species help with struc-

and is smothered with large flat heads of tiny flowers, each surrounded by a pure white circle of sterile florets. The pale green, deeply veined leaves turn red in the autumn. The snowball bush, *V. opulus* 'Sterile' looks well when treated as a wall shrub; it is tall growing and covered with huge balls of snow white flowers. *V. o.* 'Notcutts Variety' bears gorgeous translucent red berries in autumn, and with its bonus of evergreen foliage and scented flowers, *V. × burkwoodii* should certainly be considered for inclusion in the border.

In addition, *Choisya ternata*, the Mexican orange, makes a large bush, tempting for its evergreen leaves, aromatic when crushed, and sweetly scented flowers. It definitely needs shelter and a sunny spot, however.

Also indispensable in the early summer are the mock oranges, Philadelphus species. Tending to be lax and rangy, they should be sited at the rear of the border where other plants can grow up to hide the bare stems. An established plant will be covered with literally hundreds of blooms, filling the air with a delicious perfume of orange blossom. *Philadelphus* 'Belle Etoile' has large open single flowers, prominent yellow stamens and a purple blotch at the base of the petals, while *P.* 'Virginal' lets its double flowers hang in clusters.

If you have a good, cool acid soil take the opportunity to grow the beautiful though under used specimen, *Eucryphia × nymansensis*; this makes a quick growing evergreen ornamental tree bearing large cream flowers in late summer. Hardier, but slower growing, *E. glutinosa* makes an

White flowers gleam against a dense supporting cast of green foliage, their outlines silhouetted to show the immense variety of shapes. In this border starlike lilies combine with saucer-shaped cosmos, tightly packed roses and simple daisy-flowered chrysanthemums.

tural framework and their maintenance is minimal; another plus in this busy age. Once they are established, little more than the occasional light pruning is required to keep vigorous growers in shape. As this may often be done while dead-heading after flowering the task is far from arduous. Then you can just sit back and let the seasons unfold before you.

Viburnum is an extensive family of deciduous and evergreen shrubs which can provide a white flowering species for every season. Resembling a multi-tier wedding cake, *Viburnum plicatum* 'Mariesii' makes a glorious show in early summer. It grows horizontally

White berries add a distinguished dimension to a planting scheme with the winter fruiting shrub, *Symphoricarpos albus* 'White Hedge'.

elegant pyramid, flowering from July. It is semi-deciduous, and having flowered, its leaves take on an orange hue in autumn.

It is later in the summer when hydrangeas start to come into their own. They do need partial shade and deep, moist soil but they are most rewarding shrubs, providing a wide range of flower forms. The most well known are the aptly named mop-heads; this showy variety possibly looks best as a container plant to make a feature on a terrace. More elegant are the flat-headed lacecaps, a circle of pure white sterile florets ringing the flat corymb of pinkish fertile flowers. Similar in form but with unusual, large oak-shaped leaves is *H. quercifolia*, which can often give rich autumn tints. *H. paniculata* 'Grandiflora'

meanwhile is quite spectacular, with huge greenish-white panicles on long, arching stems, and wonderful as a dried flower for decoration in the house.

Whether the brilliant gold and orange of autumn foliage or the rich red of fruits and berries belong in a white garden is a moot point. In their favour, these fruits and falling leaves are an integral part of the life cycle of a garden and indeed their colours do give such pleasure before the onset of winter. If reassurance is needed, remember that shrubs like viburnum, cotoneaster and pyracantha do have white flowers as well as their autumn fruits and reddish tints; and the ornamental cherry and crab apple blossom give as fantastic a show in the spring as their display of rich fruits in autumn. Perhaps anyway, the white garden should be allowed to have its own private harvest. Imagine too a snowy white scene in December with branches of holly with bright red berries all ready to cut and bring inside to complement the fireside glow. For the purist, the winter fruits of the snowberry, *Symphoricarpos albus*, are not red but white; most striking for a table decoration.

Climbing shrubs play an important role in maintaining a focus of interest in the garden through the seasons, whether they are clothing walls or trained over pergolas or arbours. Two of the most vigorous species of clematis, *C. montana* 'Alba' and the evergreen *C. armandii* flower early in spring while soon the glorious pendulous racemes of *Wisteria sinensis* 'Alba' will take over, either against a high dark wall or smothering a pergola. There is an abundance of choice throughout the summer: scented honeysuckle and jasmine, luscious rambling and climbing roses and the larger flowering clematis, which all have a wide range of white varieties.

Some of the greatest white flowering glories of the summer months are to be found amongst the herbaceous perennials. Covered in detail later in the Planting List, these include much-loved favourites like delphinium, gypsophila and astilbe. Lesser known species are there too: the obedient plant, *physostegia*; lysimachia, eremurus and the burning bush, *Dictamnus albus*. Their role in the mixed border is to provide sheer luxuriant display with a great wealth of showy or more subtle forms appearing in succession through the season. Early on, heart-shaped blooms of dicentra hang gracefully from curving stems while a little later, clouds of delicate gypsophila might float lazily past spikes of Canterbury bells, with snapdragons and Brompton stocks to bring back memories of childhood.

The tall and graceful windflower, *Anemone japonica*, is tremendously valuable as it will flower late into autumn. For sheer delight in winter, helleborus, the Christmas and Lenten roses, produce their lovely nodding flowers, very close to the ground, when little else is around to cheer the spirits.

To keep a mixed planting scheme full and lively through the year, leave some areas free for infilling with seasonal bedding and bulbs. Pale cream wallflowers planted in late autumn will provide green leaf all winter and will bloom in the spring; tulips and daffodils set at around the same time would intermingle beautifully with them. For the front of the border, combine crocus bulbs with spring

It is always a challenge to maintain interest in the garden in winter. Evergreen shrubs have a vital part to play but some deciduous ones leave an unexpected display after their leaves have gone. For example, the blue-tinged, bare white stems of *Rubus cockburnianus* create a curiously ephemeral statement in equally bare surroundings.

polyanthus, and pansies too, now obtainable for both spring and winter flowering. Discard the flowers and lift the bulbs to rest them during the summer, replacing them with summer annuals as soon as the danger of frost is over. Giving a continuous show through summer, the tall and graceful, white and lime-green scented tobaccos, and lower growing busy lizzies are indispensable for a semi-shaded spot while petunias, stocks and white lobelia must have sun. Delightful cosmos with saucer-shaped flowers carried above a sea of ferny foliage will bloom profusely from late summer to autumn.

The White Effect

Water

A white garden will, by implication, induce an atmosphere of calm with the cooling influences of pale flowers set against lush green foliage. The presence of water, however, whether in a still pool or a splashing fountain will further enhance the relaxing ambience by introducing the dimension of tranquillity.

The soothing effect of water cannot be underestimated. Imagine a hot afternoon in a Mediterranean courtyard, a vine covered pergola overhead and a fountain gently playing. This sound alone, without the visual delight, is enough to make you forget that long, dusty walk back from the beach. Remember too how a swimming pool looks with sunlight glinting off the moving surface, tempting the onlooker to jump in and cool off; or an icy lake in the mountains, deep, dark and still, the sound of distant birds carried echoing across its surface. Wherever water occurs, whether it is wild like the sea or a river, or controlled in a lake or a pool, it exerts a powerful influence over the senses.

Water also has the ability to reflect light; a function which can be used to great effect in the garden to brighten a shady area. Its movement will catch rays of sunlight which dance and glint upon the surface or project reflections of nearby foliage. Designed in conjunction with an expanse of mirror, a further illusion of increased light and space can be created. This could be particularly relevant and beneficial in a small town garden, which may perhaps be shaded by tall trees or buildings, where as many visual tricks as possible need to be employed to capitalize on the garden's assets and maximize its potential.

Unless space and budget extend to allow for a lake or a stream, it is probably better to consider the use of water in restricted quantity. Thankfully it is not nearly so difficult to handle as at first it may seem. There are really only two basic directions to take in the deployment of water in the garden: either formal or naturalistic. Fountains figure prominently in formal designs and are relatively easy to organize: they need no special plumbing, just an electric power supply. At its simplest, all that is required to make a fountain is a water collecting device at ground level such as a small pond or a shallow dish into which an electric re-circulating pump is installed. The pump outlet is fitted with a cap which allows water to emerge as a fine spray or as a bubbly gurgle, the pressure being adjusted to meet the desired velocity or height. This is all very well as far as it goes but the results may be a little contrived.

A more elegant arrangement might incorporate a statue or urn, perhaps located in the centre of a paved area. Water would be pumped up to this and then released through an appropriate orifice to cascade or spill over gently down to the pool below. Of course, this need not be free-standing in a central site; where space is restricted, a noble lion's mask attached to a wall with a bowl underneath to collect the water, would be ideal.

Formal water features should be accompanied by quite an understated planting treatment, otherwise they become quite overwhelmed and lose their visual impact. An important role is played here by foliage as it creates a lush setting to enhance the water's cooling properties. *Alchemilla mollis*, Lady's mantle, is just the thing to foil the paved edge of a pool. It forms itself into low clumps of pale lime green leaves which are covered in the finest velvety down. These collect droplets of water which glisten on their surface in the most delightful way, its plumes of frothy greenish flowers gently adding to its subtle charm. The miniature water lily, *Nymphaea* 'Helvola', is particularly free flowering, creamy with a yellow centre; float it on the surface and let it nestle amongst its speckled olive-green leaves.

The wall fountain might be framed more dramatically by the glorious, hardy royal fern *Osmunda regalis*, with its dense arching fronds. For a fittingly grand partner, plant clumps of equally regal white arum lilies, *Zantedeschia aethiopica*.

The informal or natural water garden has an entirely different role to play and offers countless planting possibilities. Instead of making an architectural statement, it becomes an integral part of the landscaping. The planting is the important factor, the pool being a device for reflecting images and setting the scene. Plants which naturally grow beside water obviously require moist soil so the water garden must be located in a place where it will be possible to achieve this. Suitable pools can be constructed easily with the use of a heavy rubber or PVC pond liner, as shown later, in Chapter 3, along with planting ideas.

The white water garden is a most tempting idea, offering the prospect of a dense background of lush foliage like tall bamboos with

Opposite
Formality can combine with fun in the water garden. Here, two huge topiary birds sit quietly as if waiting to bathe in the dark still pool which is covered by a water lily shroud.

their rustling pale green leaves and clumps of velvety, glaucous hostas in shades of lime and blue-greens. Emerging from them to reflect and sparkle delicately on the pool's dark surface, would be drifts of creamy astilbe and filipendula, nodding heads of bright leucojum, water iris and elegant white spires of sisyrinchium.

Mirror

Creating a garden is fun and it often requires stretching the imagination. Extending its scope, dealing with difficult situations and making the most of what it has to offer, are all part of the challenge.

Sometimes, what appears to be, does not really exist. To play tricks on the eye and create illusions, the use of a mirror is invaluable. It is used extensively indoors but its application in the garden is usually unexplored. A tiny patio or pond can appear twice its size or a door in a wall can lead nowhere.

By reflecting images a mirror can apparently increase space or give an illusion of length. Placed at the end of a narrow courtyard or at the side entrance of a building, it will open up the space to give it a less claustrophobic feel. It will also reflect light, thus having an important use in opening up gloomy areas.

A small patio, perhaps below street level, would be lightened up and visually extended to double its size if one wall were covered with mirror. Climbing plants with interesting foliage, such as Virginia creeper and ornamental grape vines should be used both on the opposite wall and around the mirror to foil its edges. A few horizontal wires might be taken across above head height to train the foliage to emphasize the courtyard effect. The ubiquitous white busy Lizzie and tobacco plants once again come to the rescue in the shade, but creamy Japanese honeysuckle and pure white jasmine could clamber up to show off at high level, scenting the summer evening air. A little trompe l'oeil joke, which has been used very successfully, is the fake door. The addition of a mirror increases the effect significantly. A path leads up to a blank wall. To this is fixed a door glazed with square panes of mirror. The effect is finished by a timber arch to frame it. The illusion of a garden to enter beyond will not only extend the visual range of the garden but will fool your guests every time.

A cautionary note: specify heavy grade mirror (at least 5 mm thick) which can withstand wet conditions. To be extra sure, protect the coating on its back surface with silver foil and mount it on a wooden board. Fix it to the wall securely: a mirror crashing down on your dinner party is certainly not the effect you intended.

Lighting

One of the most precious qualities of white flowers is their ability to provide a luminous glow in the early evening and in the moonlight. This exclusive factor makes it possible to enjoy your garden way beyond the daylight hours. This may be especially relevant in the city if you are out each day working and seeing the garden more during the evening than at any other time.

Borrowed lighting, either from neighbouring houses or from street lamps, may be all that is needed to allow your flowers to come to life after dark. With the judicious use of electric garden lights, however, you can create a mystery night-time world. Do not only think of it in summer while you are enjoying cocktails or supper in the open air; in winter you can produce a fairy-tale stage set of foliage and shadow to be enjoyed from your sitting room. Imagine a Christmas scene with snow on the ground and frost covered holly branches; you could even add tiny fairy lights to sparkle in the bare branches of a tree.

Specialized lighting stores and garden centres carry a range of suitable weather proof fittings. The easiest to use are mounted on spikes to push into the ground, thus providing up-lighting from a low level. These give a pleasant floodlit effect in the background, creating lots of atmosphere and strong shadows. Down- and floodlights can be fixed to walls, buildings or trees; use them selectively to spotlight a key plant or an ornamental feature such as a statue, but do not be over-enthusiastic, as overuse of this kind of lighting leads to a sort of sports stadium effect, killing all attempts at subtlety and ambience. Play around with torch lights or builders' lamps before deciding exactly where to site your lighting; think about the overall effect you want to achieve and the vantage points from which it will be seen.

Be sure to employ a qualified electrician to install your system so that all parts are weatherproof and safe. Light switches should be situated in suitable places both outside and inside the house for ease of operation, and lights could be set on a timer to link up with a security system.

Opposite
Water is a wonderful device to create an instant and tranquil sanctuary in the garden, particularly if used in an informal setting. This woodland backdrop is reflected sympathetically in the quiet pond while a solitary figure appears immune to the charm of the creamy-white *Tulipa* 'Purissima' gleaming in dappled sunlight.

Ornament and Furniture

It will often be the special touches that lift a garden from the ordinary to the distinctive; choosing an unusual paving material like cobbles instead of pre-cast slabs, for example, or having a trellis specially made to complement the garden instead of buying something off the peg. But non-structural elements play their part too.

Strong visual and textural statements are needed to accent and reinforce a garden design. Statues or sculptures may fill this role or perhaps a carefully placed piece of furniture. They do not have to be grand or serious; frivolity and fantasy have just as much a part to play in a landscape. Selection of such a piece should be made with the atmosphere and styling of its setting in mind. It must be strong and impressive but the scale and form should relate to its surroundings. Though their primary use is to create a focal point of interest in the garden, ornamental pieces may also be used as an architectural device to balance or offset the effect of another dominant feature such as a tall tree or high wall.

The word statue seems to imply an expensive antique but many reasonably priced reproductions are available; made from concrete they can be induced to weather down quickly with the application of some liquid manure or a proprietory stone-ageing product. Figures, busts or vases would all seem to belong in a traditional garden design, be it formal or romantic. Although the work of major sculptors is often out of reach of the average pocket, this should not deter you from seeking out young contemporary artists or craftsmen to provide an original piece.

Animal and bird forms are always pleasing and are made in both stylized and naturalistic forms to blend with most settings. They can also be found in every price bracket. You might allow Canada geese to march across the lawn. Looking very convincingly like lead, they are in fact made from fibreglass and are so light that you can move them to new feeding grounds at will, to confuse and amuse your friends. Or a tall figure looking out of a dense thicket of foliage might have a suitably startling effect on turning the corner of a path.

You may have salvaged a collection of sundry architectural pieces over the years; a broken figure, some old ridge tiles from a roof, part of a fountain or maybe some rocks or large beach pebbles. Assembled to form a personal sculpture of your own memories, they could be more precious than the most expensive statue.

Plant pots need not merely be practical but can be used as semi-living visual features to punctuate a planting scheme or to give scale while a new border is growing on. Obviously effective on a terrace or patio, they can also add texture and scale if sited amongst plants in a bed. Choose from literally hundreds of designs, both traditional and contemporary. The best materials, as always, are the natural ones; terracotta and stoneware, although where the specific architectural detailing of an old house is to be followed, reproductions made from moulded concrete or re-constituted marble are often more appropriate. A very fine urn may be best left empty in order to show off its form; otherwise, you can compose a plant picture in your pot to balance its height and shape.

Furniture has both practical and aesthetic roles to play. A formal garden will look even more gracious with a Lutyens or Chippendale-style timber bench. It does not have to be white, though; experiment with a deep turquoise, sea green or Wedgwood blue. Each of these colours will appear dynamic but sophisticated, accenting varied foliage tones and setting off the white flowers.

Being relatively small, of light and neat appearance, metal furniture is ideal for eating areas. Contemporary styles made of what looks like heavy wire are very exciting, while iron strapwork and wrought-iron reproductions would stand elegantly in many settings.

Rustic timber Appalachian-style pieces, rattan and willow appear sympathetic in a casual setting but they are not necessarily weatherproof, so remember to take them under cover for the winter and in bad weather conditions.

Above left
Used succinctly, statuary and furniture provide visual relief and a focus for the eye.

Above
This white iron seat wrapped around a tree trunk reinforces the gentle white planting which might otherwise fade against the expanse of green lawn and trees.

Opposite
Creative lighting will extend the use of the garden through the evening to be enjoyed from inside or out.

White
Garden Designs

Spring Garden

If the idea of creating a white garden is appealing – but not the idea of it taking over your entire space – a one-season area could be the answer. Spring would lend itself perfectly to this application with so many early bulbs, fruit blossom and flowering shrubs available from which to make your choice.

This design shows what can be done with an outlying area which was perhaps once an orchard. It is very easy to achieve, giving a light woodland feel with a wide selection of plants including many interesting bulbs. In summer it might become a children's play area or provide a peaceful spot for picnics. It can easily be scaled down in size to make a small shrub and bulb corner.

An existing Bramley apple tree is the starting point, together with its neighbour a mature ornamental bird cherry, *Prunus padus* 'Watereri', adorned by its racemes of almond scented flowers. *P.* 'Shirotae' makes a lovely alternative, with drooping clusters of blossom and a wider spreading form. The horse chestnut, *Aesculus hippocastanum* 'Flore Pleno' is a handsome partner with long lasting white flowers and shiny conkers for the children in autumn.

A collection of flowering shrubs chosen for the variety of form and texture is grouped informally in front of the cherry tree. Rising up at the back, *Viburnum × burkwoodii* makes an evergreen linchpin for the group, producing heads of scented, waxy flowers throughout spring. Bridal wreath, *Spiraea × arguta* is an understandably popular shrub producing masses of densely covered, arching flower spikes, making a superb contrast to the compact *Rhododendron* 'Palestrina'. There are many exquisite varieties in this family, giving extravagantly beautiful clusters of bell-shaped flowers, often scented, with evergreen foliage to give a woodland background for the rest of the year.

An orchard makes a perfect setting for a spring garden with early blossom trees such as cherry and pear to serve as framework for woodland bulbs and flowers. *Ornithogalum umbellatum* is a lovely spring bulb suitable for naturalizing in short grass.

The brooms are a welcome sight in spring with dense cascades of pretty little blooms. *Cytisus × praecox* a rich cream in colour is especially vigorous, and *C. albus*, pure white with greyish leaves. Snowy mespilus, *Amelanchier canadensis*, is covered in pure white, starry flowers followed in summer by edible black fruits. It really is worth growing as in autumn it also gives a magnificent show of orangey red foliage.

A spring garden provides a wonderful opportunity to plant all those exquisite early bulbs so perfectly complementing this woodland scheme. These are best placed informally in largish groups, sweeping around the base of trees and out into the grassland. Here, a path has been mown between the trees, allowing the bulbs to naturalize in the longer grass on either side. In summer when the bulbs have died down, the whole area can be mown. In this way, they will multiply and spread with little further assistance than an application of general fertilizer in spring.

So many and varied species of gorgeous

bulbous plants are available that it would be a great shame to restrict choices to the usual crocuses and daffodils. For a successive show right through the season, a selection can be made from the following. Start out the year with a tall version of the familiar and much loved snowdrop, *Galanthus nivalis* 'S. Arnott' or the double form, 'Flore Pleno'. Confusingly similar is the spring snowflake, *Leucojum vernum*, also with green markings but with petals all of an equal size.

Of the crocuses, C. 'Snow Bunting' is a good white and 'Joan of Arc' is a larger flowered hybrid. Spikes of tiny white cape hyacinths, *Muscari botryoides album* make a refreshing change from the more common blue and to contrast, clusters of starlike flowers are carried on the stems of *Ornithogalum umbellatum*, star of Bethlehem.

The windflower, *Anemone nemorosa*, loves to grow in moist dappled shade and the massed effect of low clumps of its simple flowers is charming. The rhizomes spread quickly and it seeds freely too. Enjoying similar conditions and not to be missed at any cost is erythronium, the dog's-tooth violet. *E. dens-canis* 'White Splendour' makes a charming picture carrying its nodding flowers, 15 cm (6 in) high, above greyish-brown blotched leaves while taller, at 30 cm (12 in) with larger creamy blooms, is *E. revolutum* 'White Beauty', also with contrasting textural foliage. Nearby, plant the wake robin, *Trillium grandiflorum*. This is interesting for its pure white flowers composed of three pointed petals with three green sepals, growing from three broad bright green leaves.

It is impossible not to wax lyrical about

1. Apple seedling
2. *Prunus padus*
3. *Aesculus hippocastanum* 'Flore Pleno'
4. *Clematis montana*
5. *Virburnum × burkwoodii*
6. *Spiraea × arguta nana* 'Bridal Wreath'
7. *Rhododendron* 'Palestrina'
8. *Cytisus albus*
9. *Camellia* 'Alba Simplex'
10. *Cornus stolonifera* 'Flaviramea'
11. *Amelanchier laevis*
12. *Narcissus* 'Mount Hood'
13. *Erythronium dens-canis* 'White Splendour'
14. *Crocus* 'Joan of Arc'
15. *Leucojum vernum*
16. *Narcissus* 'Thalia'
17. *Ornithogalum umbellatum*
18. *Trillium grandiflorum*
19. *Narcissus* 'Trousseau'

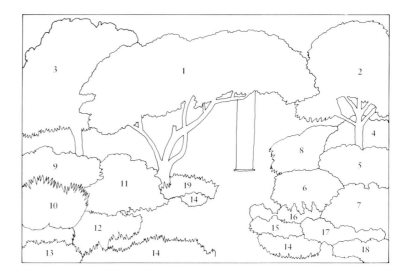

spring bulbs, especially when such delights as *Fritillaria meleagris* exist. Even though the well known chequerboard effect of the purple variety is lost, the shy nodding heads of *F. m.* 'Alba' and 'Aphrodite' are quite lovely. Remember too that the familiar woodland bluebell has a white form in *Scilla sibirica* 'Alba'.

For planting in large drifts towards the back of the garden, choose from some of the taller narcissus like 'Mount Hood' and 'Trousseau', or of medium height, 'Thalia' and 'Cheerfulness' are lovely. Tiny species such as *N. triandrus* 'Alba' would be charming nestling with the woodland plants. The small species tulips, *T. tarda*, *T. turkestanica* and *T. kaufmanniana* would have a place here too where they can be seen from the path.

Always remember that bulbs need a free draining site so incorporate extra grit or other material when planting near the moisture loving woodland plants.

Magnolia × soulangeana with its purple stained waxy flowers makes a magnificent specimen tree for a spring garden. Lime green spires of *Euphorbia wulfenii* provide stately underplanting interspersed with stems of pure white tulips.

Topiary Garden

The fashion for topiary gardens reached its height in England in the seventeenth century. The need developed for a formal garden near to the house which could be controlled and contained, quite separate from the landscape beyond. They were designed in a very rigid geometric form, usually with a surrounding hedge of evergreen yew and lower hedges of box to create intricate shapes within. The designs varied from simple squares and diamonds to intricate overlapping circles and ropes to create aptly named knot gardens. The idea progressed to incorporate large specimen trees clipped into balls and pyramids and a vogue developed in the nineteenth century for huge animals, birds and even railway engines.

These elaborate schemes took many generations to mature and are quite unsuited to today's demand for instant effect. The design here has adopted the original thesis but uses plant material which will establish quickly. It retains a formal shape but turns it sideways to create diagonal lines with green and silver hedging arranged to criss-cross, forming planting beds within.

The best box for hedging is *Buxus Sempervirens* 'Suffruticosa' which can be obtained container grown up to 20 cm (8 in) high and should be planted the same distance apart as its height. *Santolina incana* has finely incised, silvery foliage which will quickly grow into a dense hedge, or, alternatively, use lavender. The old English *Lavandula spica* 'Hidcote' is a suitably compact blue flowering variety, but purists would plant the Dutch *L. vera* 'Nana Alba' with its silvery foliage and white flowers.

To create a dense hedge quickly, plants should be trimmed back immediately after planting, then every six months until the required height and thickness has been achieved. After that an annual trim in spring should suffice to keep them in shape. These border hedges need not be higher than 25–30 cm (10–12 in).

Buxus 'Suffruticosa' is the best form of box for low topiary hedging while other varieties may be used to create pyramids, balls and other architectural forms. These designs show layouts for planting enclosures; the only limitation is your imagination.

Prepare the planting trenches well, using plenty of humus and some bonemeal. Make sure that the ground is free of perennial weeds. Water in very thoroughly after planting, making sure that each plant gets up to two gallons of water, and thereafter water regularly, especially in spring and summer, until they are well established. More new hedges fail due to lack of water than from any other cause. Apply fertilizer each spring.

Yew is shown as the ideal evergreen perimeter hedge, but Leylandii conifers could be used as a cheap, fast growing alternative. The heavy, dark green background is a perfect foil for the delicate white flowering plants selected but a beech or hornbeam hedge could look very effective with more dominant subjects.

The planting scheme has been deliberately kept simple in order to show off each type of flower in its space. The vision of the flowers is light and feathery in contrast to the solid forms of the hedges.

The lines of the hedges are continued by paths constructed of old stock bricks, infilled by gravel to maintain a soft appearance. Two pairs of specimen plants face each other across the central courtyard to focus the design. Box trees trained in a corkscrew form are planted directly in the ground, while on opposite sides, timber planters contain a lollipop-shaped bay tree, *Laurus nobilis* with a corkscrew stem. Variegated holly, *Ilex aquifolium* 'Silver Queen' could be used here as an original alternative.

Old-fashioned roses have been chosen as the taller species to grow at the back of the garden, with their rather loose habit and most beautiful blooms. The Albas are in the main, very hardy, growing well in any situation and wonderfully scented; the flower form is double with a muddled centre. 'La Virginale' is pure white and prolific, 'Jeanne d'Arc' has flowers of rich cream fading to ivory white, while 'Pompon Blanc Parfait' is a tidy growing form with long lasting pink flushed flowers. Albas produce good orange fruit.

Rosa spinosissima 'Double Cream' produces masses of double flowers followed by spectacular black fruit. 'White de Meaux' is a compact centifolia with densely packed, sweet smelling flowers. An unusual rugosa, 'Souvenir de Philémon Cochet' has a strangely complex, double form, very fragrant and perpetual flowering. 'Danae', a hybrid musk, makes an attractive bush with dark, shiny foliage. The flowers are creamy yellow in bud, fading to a soft white.

Marguerites fill the front beds and beside them is the curious and aromatic burning bush, *Dictamnus albus*. When flowering is over, the plant produces seed heads filled with a volatile oil which at the end of hot summer

1 *Dictamnus albus* (Burning bush)
2 *Chrysanthemum frutescens* (Marguerite)
3 *Buxus sempervirens* (Box)
4 *Santolina incana* (Cotton lavender)
5 *Buxus sempervirens* 'Suffruticosa' (Box hedging)
6 *Gypsophila paniculata* 'Compacta Plena' (Baby's breath)
7 *Rosa* 'Pompon Blanc Parfait' (Alba rose)
8 *Rosa* 'La Virginale' (Alba rose)
9 *Rosa spinosissima* 'Double Cream' (Scotch rose)
10 *Cosmos bipinnatus* 'White Sensation' (Cosmea)
11 *Laurus nobilis* (Bay)
12 *Taxus baccata* (Yew)

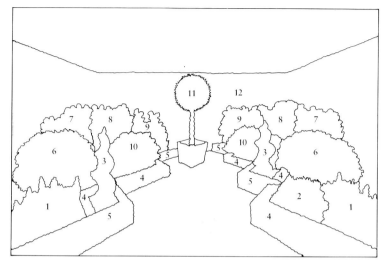

days may be ignited, creating a blue flame; a spectacular planting dimension.

Clouds of tiny-flowered baby's breath fill the centre beds, blooming throughout the summer. Behind them rise the equally ephemeral *Cosmos bipinnatus* 'White Sensation'. In late summer, through the autumn, this lovely plant produces masses of huge single flowers, which appear to float above a sea of feathery green foliage.

Although these plants bloom in summer, it is perfectly possible to extend the flowering season to start early in spring. The marguerites are not hardy and should be lifted at the end of the season as should the annual cosmos. Replace them in autumn with elegant lily-flowered tulips, narcissus and jonquils. Complete the picture with creamy, scented wallflowers planted late in the year after the perennial gypsophila have died down and removed after flowering, before summer.

The severity of this restrained design is challenged by the exuberant clump of bright white lily-flowered tulips. In summer, a standard form marguerite tree would make a similarly dashing effect.

Herbaceous Border

This is a garden to inspire the enthusiastic beginner and to delight the experienced plantsperson. It provides the opportunity to grow a huge selection of plants without the constraints of a formal design, simply for the sheer enjoyment of their beauty and variety. Its strength is in the sheer volume of plants, each one demanding its space, though anxious to meet up with its neighbours. There are plenty of old favourites with some less common species featuring too, but it is, of course, just a stepping off point to all the wonderful and unusual varieties to be found.

It has been arranged as two long beds with a high hedge in the background to provide both shelter and visual contrast. A path of stone slabs, interplanted with sweet-smelling camomile and white flowering thrift curves gently through to a voluptuous, Lutyens style seat from which to contemplate the vista. The arrangement is informal, but plants have been positioned carefully to allow for contrasts of height and texture. Though taller, spreading varieties appear mainly at the back of the border, with graduation down to low edging plants by the path, the scheme is made more dramatic and eye-catching by siting high flowering spires such as veronica and campanula centrally amongst low growing species. Dramatically successful architectural punctuation marks can also be introduced with huge spikes of artichoke heads emerging from a mass of deeply cut, sculptural leaves.

Do remember always to plant in strong statements with smaller varieties grouped in clumps or drifts for impact. Though the intention is for the finished result to appear full and overflowing, enough space should be allowed for the plants to establish themselves and for them to receive plenty of light and air. Trial and error may be involved in the first year or two, especially if you are a relative newcomer to gardening and need to get to know your plants.

When planning a border, balance shape and form with time of flowering and plant boldly to achieve full effect through spring and summer. Tall flowering *Spiraea × arguta nana* make a superb backdrop while delphiniums are good punctuation marks.

If you find that one plant obscures the view to another, or if something spreads much further than its description has implied, it is usually quite in order to dig it up and move it to another spot.

Generally speaking, the group of plants known as herbaceous perennials, comprises reasonably or totally hardy species which start growing in spring with the leaves and flowers dying back completely by winter, then reappearing the following spring. They grow up very quickly and often achieve great height and volume, with the benefit of fresh, new foliage every year. This pattern does, however, incur a great deal of maintenance in terms of staking and tying as they develop, with the subsequent clearing away at the end of the season. It should be considered, though, that all this work is more than amply repaid by the generous and unstinting show that these plants provide.

In today's terms, with time and space in short supply, it is not usually desirable to allow an entire area to be bare of plants throughout the winter, so this contemporary version of the herbaceous border incorporates shrubs and bulbs to help it through the leaner months. Hydrangea and viburnum offer many white flowering species, with a good variety of leaf and flower forms while philadelphus or choisya will give orange-blossom scents when they bloom.

Variegated shrubs like *Cornus alba* and *C. controversa* will fill a large space with gleaming, white-edged foliage, though their flowers are insignificant. Shrub roses, large and small, give an infinite range of perfumed flowers throughout the summer and provide an excellent link between the perennials and more densely growing shrubs.

Temporary bedding such as wallflowers and pansies can be combined with tulips and daffodils to bloom in spring, occupying the empty spaces before the main growing season commences. In summer, tobaccos, petunias and impatiens would help to fill out a newly established site.

Your plant stock can be increased easily, and only at the cost of time and a little effort, by lifting and dividing perennials after they have died back in autumn/winter. Replant them immediately before they dry out. Do check first that they are suitable for this treatment though, as certain species, such as peonies, must not be disturbed once established.

An open and sunny, well-drained site with good soil is required to get the best results from this kind of garden and a thick mulch of forest bark or leaf mould applied in spring before annual weeds appear will help to

1 *Rosa* 'Gloire de Dijon'
2 *Rosa* 'Boule de Neige
3 *Rosa* 'Blanche Double de Coubert'
4 *Rosa* 'Ballerina'
5 *Cytisus purpureus albus*
6 *Gypsophila paniculata*
7 *Lupinus* 'Blushing Bride'
8 *Lilium regale*
9 *Veronica virginica* 'Alba'
10 *Sorbaria aitchisonii*
11 *Hydrangea aborifolia*
12 *Campanula pyramidalis alba*
13 *Penstemon barbatus* 'Alba'
14 *Convolvulus cneorum*
15 *Lysimachia clethroides*
16 *Hemerocallis*
17 *Thalictrum aquilegiifolium album*
18 *Clematis recta*
19 *Cornus alba* 'Elegantissima'
20 *Polemonium caeruleum album*
21 *Potentilla* 'Vilmoriniana'
22 *Cistus* × *corbariensis*
23 *Galtonia candicans*
24 *Arenaria balearica*
25 *Tiarella cordifolia*
26 *Helleborus orientalis*
27 *Cynara scolymus* 'Glauca'
28 *Hosta sieboldiana* 'Elegans'
29 *Saxifraga umbrosa*
30 *Dimorphotheca aurantiaca* 'Glistening White'
31 *Lavandula vera* 'Alba'
32 *Anthemis tinctoria*
33 *Hebe albicans*
34 *Filipendula hexapetala*
35 *Viola*
36 *Alyssum maritimum*

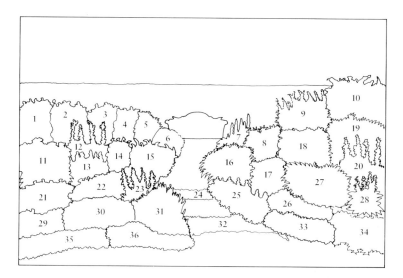

conserve moisture and keep weeds at bay. Fork in an application of general fertilizer first to help the new season's growth. Stake tall growing species firmly, but as informally as possible, using natural twigs and branches. The overall effect is intended to be riotous and full, so allow the plants to grow together taking the space they need for a relaxed and flowing show of leaf and flower.

A vine covered pergola and cool green lawn make calm surroundings for a white and grey theme. The herbaceous *Clematis recta* with sweetly scented flowers would be suitable in such an overflowing border.

Walled Garden

A walled garden offers a unique cultural environment providing shelter from cold winds and creating a microclimate in which tender plants can thrive with increasing flowering potential for all species. Plants which might otherwise have to be grown in a glasshouse can be grown on a warmth-absorbing south or west wall, even allowing a crop of peaches to be produced. In fact, all fruit trees, trained espalier fashion on a wall, will crop earlier and more heavily than in a free standing situation. Such a garden can also make a cosy and intimate space with great scope for a magical planting design incorporating a mass of delightfully overflowing climbers, covered in flowers for a substantial part of the year.

This is primarily a romantic design, incorporating as it does, the wisteria arbour, but practical thoughts of the kitchen are never far away, with fruit trees and herbs being given pride of place. Natural brick is the most traditional construction material for walls, but may not always be available or aesthetically appropriate so cement-rendered blockwork has been shown here to demonstrate its possibilities. To make it appear sympathetic to the garden, it has been painted a warm ochre which provides a gentle contrast to the white flowers, and would lend a mellow and relaxing ambience, even on a gloomy day.

The intention is to enclose the space entirely with plants, including as many climbers as possible. These not only cover the walls but twine around and flower at a higher level, creating a swag-like effect. The east facing wall boasts a fan-trained Morello cherry which prefers this cooler aspect with self-clinging *Hydrangea petiolaris* beyond it to flower in early summer. Opposite, a peach enjoys the benefit of the warm west wall. An unusual wall shrub, related and similar to the hydrangea, is growing beside it; *Schizophragma integrifolium* is also self-clinging but the flat cymes of flowers appear later, from mid-summer onwards.

Above
Wisteria is the most graceful of climbing shrubs. *W. floribunda* 'Alba' is a vigorous form which is seen at its best growing over a pergola where its huge drooping racemes can be shown to advantage.

Above right
A walled garden not only provides shelter for tender plant species but also creates a perfect setting for a quiet arbour. This one, constructured of slatted timber, is practically smothered with the climbing *Rosa* 'Iceberg' set off well by the vine covered wall and clumps of *Alchemilla mollis* at its feet and spikes of Canterbury bells, *Campanula medium*, at the other side.

A rustic timber pergola almost smothered with huge pendent racemes of pure white wisteria in spring, surrounds a sympathetic seat, shading it from hot summer sun with masses of delicate, pale green foliage. Dark glossy leaved camellias frame it on either side, offering exquisite blooms at the end of winter.

The Rambling Rector rose which will quickly cover a large wall, has been selected for its profusion of small, creamy blooms and highly developed musk fragrance, with climbing Mme. Alfred Carrière on the other side, freely producing large, fragrant flowers over a long period. *Rosa brunonii*, though generally tender, would thrive in this sheltered situation, and is worth growing for its clusters of large, highly scented, single blooms and attractive greyish foliage.

The planting borders in this garden have been kept fairly narrow to show off the wall shrubs, so generally, medium to low growing species such as *Potentilla fruticosa* have been employed around their base. At the corners, where the beds widen, there is the opportunity for slightly taller shrubs. A non-fruiting member of the raspberry family, *Rubus × tridel* 'Benenden', with single saucer-shaped flowers in spring, grows up vigorously beside the cherry and advantage has been taken of the west wall to grow the lovely, but tender, tree poppy, *Romneya coulteri* with its sparkling papery white blooms. The sun loving *Lavatera trimestris* 'Alba' would be a good alternative here.

There is still plenty of room for herbaceous perennials with seasonal bedding and bulbs too, if desired. In the sunny border, densely packed stocks nestle down with white lobelia and tiny *Bellis perennis* daisies. Also daisy-flowered, *Anthemis cupaniana* and *Artemisia nutans* 'Silver Queen' both have silver-grey foliage and thrive in full sun. They contrast well with the white flowered alyssum and arabis for ground cover, and the exquisite *Geranium sanguineum* 'Album' spilling over the path.

Over on the shady side, creamy panicles of tiny blossoms rise on spikes above the huge, bright green leaves of *Rodgersia tabularis*, with a hardy fuchsia behind. Accompanied by the sweetly scented woodruff, *Asperula odorata*, dangling bells of Solomon's seal, *Polygonatum biflorum* and diminutive white muscari, a gentle woodland feel is suggested.

The central bed has been given over totally to culinary herbs of which there are many to choose, according to individual taste and preference. Tall growing, evergreen rosemary forms the central feature, surrounded by a selection of the basics which might include

1 *Rosa* 'Madame Alfred Carrière'
2 *Rosa* 'Rambling Rector'
3 *Clematis sibirica* 'White Moth'
4 *Jasminum officinale*
5 *Prunus persica* 'Peregrine'
6 *Prunus cerasus* 'Morello'
7 *Camellia* 'Alba Simplex'
8 *Wisteria sinensis* 'Alba'
9 *Schizophragma integrifolium*
10 *Hydrangea petiolaris*
11 *Romneya coulteri*
12 *Potentilla* 'Vilmoriniana'
13 *Matthiola* 'Perpetual White'
14 *Lobelia erinus* 'Snowball'
15 *Polygonatum biflorum*
16 *Malva moschata alba*
17 *Lathyrus latifolius* 'White Pearl'
18 *Artemisia nutans* 'Silver Queen'
19 *Alyssum maritimum* 'Snowcloth'
20 *Bellis perennis* 'Monstrosa White'
21 *Asperula odorata*
22 *Vinca minor alba*
23 *Fuchsia magellanica* 'Alba'
24 *Anthemis cupaniana*
25 *Arabis caucasica* 'Flore Pleno'
26 *Geranium sanguineum album*
27 *Muscari botryoides album*
28 *Rodgersia tabularis*
29 *Rosmarinus officinalis albus*
30 *Anthemis nobilis*
31 *Allium schoenoprasum*
32 *Lavandula* 'Nana Alba'
33 *Origanum majorana*
34 *Thymus serpyllum albus*
35 *Rubus tridel* 'Benenden'

thyme, sage, oregano or marjoram, chives, tarragon and dill. Mint is rather too invasive for planting in a bed and should be restricted in a pot. Tender annuals such as basil, should only be planted out when summer days have finally warmed up.

The major element of maintenance in this garden relates to the climbers and wall shrubs which need to be trained in carefully as they grow. The most efficient and unobtrusive form of plant support is to be achieved by stretching strong wires horizontally across the walls. They should be positioned at 30–45 cm (12–18 in) centres and fixed with metal 'wall eye' hooks specially made for the purpose. It is the one area of shrub growing where pruning is exceptionally important, both to increase the flower and fruit production and to avoid an overgrown and tangled mass of stems. Specialist advice should be taken to suit individual species.

Solanum jasminoides 'Album' is a deliciously pretty climbing member of the potato family. It is quite tender so enjoys the protection of a sunny walled garden.

Water Garden

In a perfect world, every garden would be blessed with a free flowing stream alongside which to grow graceful arums and delicate astilbes. In reality, though nature may not have placed it there, the possibility exists to create a water garden in almost all situations. The sight and sound of moving water is difficult to achieve in a naturalistic manner and the simplest way to bring water into the garden would be in a still pool around which to establish a border of moisture loving species.

In this design, a small but flamboyant water garden has been located quite near to the house with stone steps leading down gently through a luxurious mix of handsome foliage to a sybaritic retreat below. The accent here is definitely one of drama and decadence with a bubbling hot tub the ultimate delight to reward the white garden adventurer.

The pool has been excavated to create a sunken garden below a paved terrace. The resulting gently sloping bank is densely planted with a bold mixture of foliage and flowering material, all of which thrives in moist soil and aspects ranging from full sun to dappled shade.

A heavy duty plastic liner covers the base of the pond, held in position at the sides by large flat stones, disguised later by the perimeter planting. The maximum water depth is 45 cm (18 in), becoming shallower towards the sides. To improve water retention, extra peat has been incorporated into the topsoil and planting on the slope is organized in a terraced manner to prevent undue soil erosion.

As a screen from the terrace beyond, a large clump of tall growing bamboo, *Phyllostachys nigra*, shelters the tub from onlookers. Its shiny black stems give it an exotic appearance which is complemented by the giant Himalayan lily, *Cardiocrinum giganteum*, growing up to 2.7 m (9 ft) tall with scented bell-shaped blooms. The kidney-shaped leaves of *Petasites japonicus* and the foliage of various hostas lap over the tub.

Above
The bog arum, *Lysichiton camtschatcensis* makes a lush and exotic feature for the edge of a pool or stream.

Above right
For larger ponds, the vigorous water hawthorn, *Aponogeton distachyos*, makes an interesting alternative to water lilies. It produces its delicate spikes of white flowers above a carpet of dark leaves for most of the year.

At the top of the garden bank, the bold form of *Fatsia japonica* provides a strong and evergreen background for spires of sisyrinchium and bold spathes of arum lilies growing at the water's edge. Clumps of dense ferns are relieved by summer planting of busy Lizzie while iberis cascades over the stone steps.

Contrasts of texture and form have been selected to complete the poolside planting. *Astilbe × arendsii* 'White Gloria' makes 60 cm (2 ft) heads of fluffy flowers with feathery foliage to match, but if space allows, plant the amazing *A. grandis* with huge inflorescences on 1.5 m (5 ft) stems.

The iris family provides some absolutely beautiful flower forms and the beardless moisture-loving species are no exception. *I. kaempferi*, 90 cm (3 ft) high with a yellow stripe, *I. laevigata* 'Alba' and *I.* 'White Swirl' rise elegantly from the edge or the water.

Low growing bergenias and leucojums mingle with delightful primulas, all enjoying the conditions of moisture and dappled shade. Choose from the fragrant *Primula reidii* with ivory pendent bell-shaped flowers, the larger Japanese *P. sieboldii*, pompom headed *P. denticulata alba* and the tall growing candelabra form, *P. japonica* 'Postford White'.

Gentle grasses make very natural poolside companions, their fine leaves and graceful forms reflected in the water. *Phalaris arundinacea* 'Picta' adds interest with its narrow leaves variegated with cream and bright green stripes and the similar *Glyceria maxima* 'Variegata' is as happy growing directly in water as in soil. Sedges with their triangular stems like *Carex pendula* or the delightful bright yellow *C. stricta* 'Bowles' Golden' do well beside pools too.

No self respecting pool would be without a liberal sprinkling of water lilies. *Nymphaea* 'Marliacea Albida' is a reliable and prolific flowerer producing gorgeous pure white blooms. The miniature *N. × helvola* produces masses of creamy flowers with textural red speckled, olive green leaves; it must only be grown in shallow water and does best in a warmer place.

This is a relatively low maintenance scheme which is to be seen at its best from spring to late summer. The black bamboo and evergreen fatsia will carry it through to winter, but most species are herbaceous perennials which should be cut back and tidied before winter. A thick mulch of forest bark chippings or peat applied in spring will help to conserve moisture during the summer.

The water surface must be kept clear of falling leaves and other debris and the water

1 *Petasites japonicus*
2 *Cardiocrinum giganteum*
3 *Phyllostachys nigra* (Black-stemmed bamboo)
4 *Dryopteris filix-mas*
5 *Hosta crispula*
6 *Hosta sieboldiana* 'Elegans'
7 *Houttuynia cordata*
8 *Phyllitis scolopendrium*
9 *Luzula maxima*
10 *Sedum album*
11 *Iberis sempervirens* 'Snowflake'
12 *Helxine soleirolii*
13 *Arenaria balearica*
14 *Vinca minor alba*
15 *Galanthus nivalis*
16 *Impatiens*
17 *Impatiens*
18 *Phyllitis scolopendrium*
19 *Athyrium filix-femina*
20 *Convallaria majalis*
21 *Fatsia japonica* (Castor oil plant)
22 *Sysirinchium striatum*
23 *Zantedeschia aethiopica* 'Crowborough' (Arum lily)
24 *Nymphaea* 'Marliacea Albida' (Water lily)
25 *Astilbe × arendsii* 'White Gloria'
26 *Primula denticulata*
27 *Leucojum aestivum*
28 *Iris spp.*
29 *Bergenia* 'Silberlicht'
30 *Eriophorum polystachion*
31 *Phalaris arundinacea picta*

Relaxed perimeter planting softens the encircling paved path around a formal pool, with much use made of arching, linear foliage and delicate flowers. Water lily leaves lie quietly waiting for their exotic blooms to appear later in summer.

level may need to be topped up from time to time if excessive evaporation occurs during the summer. The electric pump and filters for the hot tub are located at the side of it with a removable timber decking lid for access.

Needless to say, a hot tub is not obligatory, but a successful moving water effect could be achieved substituting it with a construction of large rocks and stones. Water can be made to ripple down gently into the pool by means of a simple hose and circulating pump.

City Garden

Many things are expected of a garden in the city. It should be a tranquil retreat from the busy world outside, it should afford privacy from neighbours and it will probably be expected to perform as an outside entertaining area. It is quite probable that space is severely limited and that there is a lot of shade from nearby buildings. It may also be situated below street level which may be a bonus from the privacy angle but a distinct disadvantage from the point of view of sunlight.

Shown here is a clean contemporary design in a relatively small space, using sympathetic natural materials throughout. It is completely enclosed by a high timber fence, finished in a dark coloured wood preserving stain. The planting beds have been built up above ground level to gain as much light as possible and are held by retaining walls of heavy timbers set vertically into the ground. Flat wooden slabs fixed to the wall form a simple seating system beside the barbecue; this is a permanent fixture made from stone to minimize any fire risk. Seasoned timber has again been used for the decking floor, but stone slabs or ceramic tiles would make an equally good finish. Modified to take account of weight, this design could be adapted to suit a roof terrace.

It is worth considering the installation of permanent lighting, which will not only extend the number of hours you can spend in the garden, but will also enhance its appearance as viewed from the house. Simple lamps are fixed on stakes to be set in the ground amongst the plants, creating pools of light, but wall lamps can be very effective too.

In choosing the plants for this scheme, a careful balance has been made between evergreen and deciduous varieties so that the garden will look presentable through the winter months. It is not the intention to cover the fence entirely with climbers, but rather to show off specimens against it to achieve a cool and somewhat restrained effect.

An oriental flavour is evoked in this city garden with a background of fine leaved bamboo and a bronze carp statue. Chinese blue-glazed planters are filled with chrysanthemum, erica, hebe, *Campanula isophylla* and tuberous begonias.

Elegant and densely growing black bamboo, *Phyllostachys nigra*, provides a background with clumps of grassy festuca at its base to follow the graceful form. Next to it, bearing gloriously perfumed, early summer flowers, is a white lilac tree. The clear white, mallow flowered *Abutilon vitifolium album* looks sensational in summer against the dark wood, the effect made even more beautiful with glistening *Convolvulus cneorum* at its feet. These tender species both benefit from the warm and sheltered situation. Sun-loving rock roses like tall *Cistus ladanifer* or the lower spreading *C. × corbariensis*, accompanied perhaps by prostrate silver thyme, would also work well in this sunny corner.

Cobaea scandens alba is a most unusual, but vigorous climber. Often called the cup and saucer vine, it produces strange green and white flowers until very late in the year; not fully hardy, it is usually treated as an annual. Beside it, the delicate *Solanum jasminoides* 'Album' produces masses of tiny white, star-like blossoms from mid to late summer.

Hydrangea petiolaris is the main wall shrub

on the shadier side of the garden with *Viburnum plicatum* 'Mariesii' rising in tiers of white flowers, beside it. Much attention is given to foliage in the left border to give interest in a shady area unsuitable for growing flowers. The leaves of the evergreen *Pieris japonica* are brilliant red when young and are followed by lovely drooping and heavily scented racemes of tiny white bells. Combined with the variegated evergreen *Euonymus* 'Emerald Gaiety', they make a good partnership with perennials such as glaucous, lime and grey leaved hostas and mounds of green flowered *Alchemilla mollis*.

This garden has a subtle Japanese influence and the planted 'water effect' makes an unusual feature in a semi-circular bed. A large terracotta urn is the focal point; it is placed on its side and planted with creeping, white flowered arenaria to give the illusion of water flowing from the opening. Carefully placed stones emphasize the impression of a river bed and are interplanted with clumps of evergreen ferns, delicate 'Green Spot' irises, spring flowering primulas and dwarf kaufmanniana tulips.

To enable extra flowers to be grown in this limited planting area groups of pots have been introduced. These can be replanted with bedding plants each season to provide a lively and ever changing display. Marguerites, zonal and ivy-leaf pelargoniums, petunias and Cape marigolds all deserve their place in the sun in summer, while impatiens, tobacco plants, fuchsias and campanula are all good for the shade. Tulips, daffodils, polyanthus and pansies will cheer up early spring while in autumn and winter, chrysanthemum and

1 *Alchemilla mollis*
2 *Hosta sieboldiana*
3 *Pieris japonica*
4 *Erica carnea* 'Springwood White'
5 *Erica × darleyensis* 'Silberschmelze'
6 *Viburnum plicatum* 'Mariesii'
7 *Pernettya mucronata* 'White Pearl'
8 *Cornus canadensis*
9 *Rhododendron yakushimanum*
10 *Convallaria majalis*
11 *Phyllostachys nigra*
12 *Festuca glauca*
13 *Hedera canariensis* 'Gloire de Marengo'
14 *Syringa vulgaris* 'Madame Lemoine'
15 *Convolvulus cneorum*
16 *Abutilon vitifolium album*
17 *Iris* 'Bright White'
18 *Iris* 'Green Spot'
19 *Arenaria balearica*
20 *Tulipa kaufmanniana*
21 *Primula sieboldii alba*
22 *Primula denticulata*
23 *Cobaea scandens alba*
24 *Solanum jasminoides*
25 *Cistus laurifolius*
26 *Thymus serpyllum albus*
27 *Pelargonium* 'Hermione'
28 *Hedera helix* 'Poetica'
29 *Senecio greyi*
30 *Impatiens*
31 *Chrysanthemum frutescens*
32 *Armeria maritima* 'Alba'
33 *Pelargonium peltatum* 'L'Elégante'
34 *Helichrysum petiolatum*

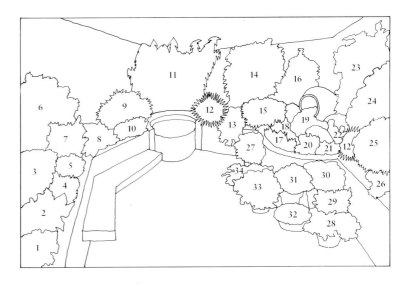

In a shady garden make plenty of use of evergreen foliage to give a year round background display. A collection of rounded box trees mingles well here with spikey euphorbia and soft fronds of fern, while the surrounding trellis is swathed with dark ivies.

heather might be teamed with evergreen euonymus or trailing ivies.

This is a very low maintenance scheme with little, if any, pruning required. Climbers need to be tied in and cut back in winter and perennials must be cleared away when they die down at the end of the year. Do make sure that plants in pots are watered daily in summer and feed and dead-head regularly to promote continuous flowering.

Conservatory

Those passionate plantsmen, the Victorians, had some extremely progressive and inventive ideas to make their ambitions flourish. Following on from the grand estates of the seventeenth century and the idea of the orangery, primarily devised for the protection of citrus fruit trees during frosty winters, came the conservatory.

The skilled British engineers of the nineteenth century built immense structures of glass and iron in which to grow tender species brought back with them from their frequent plant hunting forays all over the globe. Much to the amusement of country folk, glass conservatories were actually being built on the rooftops of tall London houses, though alas, none survive today. We are however blessed with their marvellous legacies in the botanical gardens at Kew and Glasgow, and there are many more elsewhere.

This conservatory building tradition is seeing a new lease of life today. With space becoming scarce, land and construction costs rocketing, they make a simple way of extending the home. Many companies provide a range of elaborate Victorian style creations with complicated glazing designs and many decorative accoutrements. These may not, however, suit your home or the scale of your budget.

This design shows a very simple 'lean-to' style of garden room. It could be made at a very reasonable price by a builder or the form could be developed by an architect using superior detailing and construction materials. Its clean lines provide a perfect space for the plants and a wall is available for the training of climbers.

The advantages of having a light warm room to use all the year round go without saying. However, for the plantsperson who has to live with frosty winters, it provides the opportunity to grow all those tender species from the temperate and tropical regions of the world.

Above
A heated conservatory makes the perfect excuse to create a tropical planting scheme. Huge leaved banana plants and a tall tree fern provide a foliage background for a wealth of lovely flowers such as hibiscus and plumbago with perfumed gardenias, trumpet lilies and orange blossom.

Above right
In this Victorian style conservatory, a pretty wire jardiniere overflows with trailing ivy and white primulas with *Spathyphyllum* 'Mauna Loa' showing its graceful spathe-like blooms alongside. Large and small leaved tropical fig trees provide an atmospheric evergreen framework.

Glossy leaved camellia bushes would vie for space with lemon trees and oleander, climbing bougainvillea with scented jasmine. Pushing the temperature up a little, more exotic creatures could join in. Heavily perfumed gardenias, pendulous angels' trumpets, flamboyant hibiscus and twining diplandenia would delight the eye and senses right through the year. Intersperse these with delicate ferns and tall, grassy papyrus or set them off by the huge leaves of bananas and fan palms, and it is easy to create a secret paradise garden.

Because this is an environment of glass and plain walls, foliage plays an important part in the planting design. Walls can be covered with trellis, or, more subtly, horizontal wires could be used to train climbers such as trachelospermum, jasmine and passiflora. Of course, walls need not be white. Traditional colours would be honeyed terracotta or pale sea green, which would lend a tranquil air, but if you have a taste for the dramatic, go for California hot

pink or a deep Moroccan blue to make a stunning backdrop for exotic foliage and heavily scented tropical flowers.

Scale and framework are, as always, very important. One tall growing tree such as a Phoenix palm, an olive or lemon might provide the focal point with smaller growing shrubs and flowers arranged in pots around it. These can be moved around according to their season or, in the case of some temperate species like citrus and lantana, be moved outside into the cooler, fresh air of the garden in summer.

If it is possible to arrange, build in at least one large planting bed in which vigorous climbers and large shrubs can grow unchecked by the restrictions of a pot in which they might dry out too quickly or become rootbound. This should be of a minimum depth of 60 cm (2 ft), free draining below and with 15 cm (6 in) of pebbles for drainage at the bottom. The planting medium should be a sterilized loam with extra peat and sand added, with a slightly acid balance.

Conservatories have great advantages but like all the best things in life, have their problems too. They get very hot in summer but also very cold in winter so some form of heating must be provided which can run during the night as well as in the day. For this reason, it is not always suitable to run it from the domestic heating supply if this is timed to go off at night. Broadly speaking, allow for a minimum winter night-time temperature of 4 °C for temperate plants and 8–10 °C for tropical varieties. Do install blinds when the conservatory is built; without them it will be impossibly hot for both plants and people.

1 *Hibiscus rosa sinensis*
2 *Citrus limon*
3 *Nerium oleander*
4 *Leptospermum scorparium*
5 *Gardenia jasminoides*
6 *Nephrolepis exaltata*
7 *Lantana camara* 'Snow Queen'
8 *Clerodendrum thomsoniae*
9 *Bougainvillea*
10 *Jasminum polyanthemum*
11 *Lonicera hildebrandiana*
12 *Passiflora caerulea*
13 *Astrophytum*
14 *Agave americana*
15 *Lophophora williamsii*

Provide opening vents at low and high level to allow a chimney effect pulling cooler fresh air in at the bottom and letting hot air escape at the top. Efficient ventilation is tremendously important, otherwise heat will build up, drying out the plants and encouraging glass-house pests to multiply.

There is nothing that the bugs like better than a hot, dry atmosphere. Red spider mite, mealy bugs and whitefly will become your most fearful enemy so try to keep them at bay by good housekeeping. Clear out any debris of dead leaves too and prune out weak or dying stems. Watch like a hawk for strangely spotty, pale leaves or fine webbing on the underside of foliage which indicate the presence of red spider mite. Sticky cotton wool deposits mean that mealy bug is around and if when a plant is touched, fluttering clouds appear, an infest-ation of white fly has occurred. A sticky residue, often accompanied by sooty foliage is the result of scale insect which is particularly fond of ficus trees and often the harder leaved varieties of ferns.

There are organic soap-based pesticides on the market which might prove effective against mealy bug, and natural predators can be obtained to fight red spider and white fly. These are both extremely difficult to eradicate though, so if ecological methods fail you may be forced to resort to chemical warfare.

Ensure that there is a water point on hand and damp down floors frequently in hot weather to create humidity. Because of the high levels of light and heat, pots will dry out very quickly indeed so should be checked daily. Place drip trays under them to stop any ensuing floods. Watering is best carried out in the evening and plants should be misted over on warm nights after the sun has gone down. Never water in full sun when leaves would be damaged by scorching.

Patio and Windowbox

If the idea of turning your whole garden white seems too drastic, or indeed if you have no real garden, then why not turn to pots and make a splash on a patio, balcony or roof terrace. Group them together in a mass of different heights and shapes to achieve the greatest effect, then fill each one to bursting with a selection of flowering shrubs, climbers and annuals. Change them according to the seasons, not forgetting that you will have to plant bulbs in the autumn if you want them to flower the following spring. It is really important not to be mean with pot planting; it is far better to reduce the number of containers than the number of plants in them.

The most unpromising location can be brought alive by the abundant use of pots and containers. If you have a small basement 'area' at the front of the house why not run a succession of simple terracotta pots filled with flowers down the steps. Hang wire baskets from brackets fixed to the house wall and fill them with a mixture of ivy-leaf geraniums and petunias if there is enough sun, or pendulous fuchsias and trailing ivy if not. To achieve a really full effect, plant right round the underneath as well as on top. Line the basket with a thick layer of sphagnum moss, then fill up with a good loam based compost. Prise apart the wires, carefully insert the rootball of the plant, then close them back parallel again to secure it in position. Mature seedlings are easiest to plant in this way but will take longer to establish than full grown plants.

A lovely effect can be achieved by planting an entire basket with white lobelia; the established result is a very elegant complete ball of delicate blooms. Always bear in mind that hanging baskets are very demanding as they need to be watered thoroughly every day in summer, even morning and night in a very sunny location, but the ravishing display they can give is well worth the effort.

Above
Every inch of space is precious in today's crowded world and a roof terrace makes a sun-filled hideaway in the city. Mexican orange blossom, *Choisya ternata*, makes a superb tub feature combined with white flowering *Clematis armandii* clambering behind on the trellis to make an evergreen corner. Blue decking with a cobbled infill set them perfectly into place.

Above right
The use of pots provides a versatile base for an ever-changing planting design. Flowers may be replaced each season and containers grouped according to desired effect.

Many climbers can be grown successfully in containers as long as these are large and deep enough to allow roots to develop properly so as not to inhibit growth of the plant. Weekly feeding and almost daily watering in summer are essential to keep growth sturdy. Virginia creeper, *Parthenocissus quinquefolia,* makes an excellent foliage backdrop for white flowers. It is self-clinging and as it grows, the new shoots trail down, giving a delightful curtain effect if allowed to hang over from a balcony or trellis. The deep green summer foliage turns to the richest golden red in autumn. For a good evergreen background, choose from the many climbing ivies, both dark green and variegated with white or yellow.

The vigorous passion flower will quickly cover a sunny wall; *Passiflora caerulea* 'Constance Elliott' is a pure white form of this strange and exotic flower, somewhat reminiscent of a tropical sea anemone. There are varieties of white clematis to bloom at most times of the year with jasmine and creamy honeysuckles to perfume summer evenings.

Window sills provide an excellent way of jollying up the plainest house. The sight of window boxes in a shady street, bursting with startling white buzy Lizzie, would have passers-by crossing over for a closer look. Their petals look like the purest angel frosting and appear particularly glowing at the end of the day. These are thirsty creatures needing plenty of space for their roots and rich moist soil. However, they are self dead-heading and will flower continuously from late spring until the first frost in the most dubious situations.

The choice of planting containers can be quite bewildering but whatever the design, natural materials always tend to look best. The warm, deep tones of terracotta set off white flowers beautifully and are available in both traditional and modern designs to suit your style.

Wooden beer casks sawn in half make exceptionally economical, good looking planters, the larger sizes being eminently suitable for vigorous shrubs and climbers. See if you can obtain them cut to your own specification, then make them in a succession of heights from a full barrel down to a very shallow one and arrange them like a stepped terrace. They might be painted a subtle olive green with the metal bands picked out in black, or in azure blue for a Mediterranean

1 *Rosa* 'Alister Stella Gray'
2 *Nicotiana alata* 'Cream Sensation'
3 *Nemophila maculata*
4 *Dimorphotheca aurantiaca* 'Glistening White'
5 *Euphorbia amygdaloides robbiae*
6 *Cordyline indivisa*
7 *Pelargonium* × *hortorum* 'Hermione'
8 *Impatiens* 'White Imp'
9 *Chrysanthemum frutescens*
10 *Hydrangea arborescens*
11 *Clematis* 'Henryi'
12 *Hydrangea petiolaris*
13 *Helichrysum petiolatum*
14 *Pelargonium peltatum* 'Seagull'

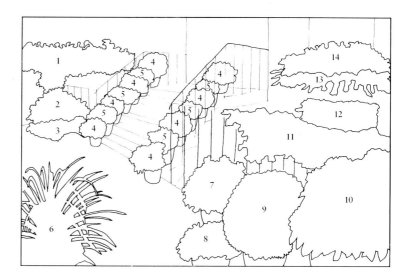

look; sensational when filled with white and silver plants.

For a contemporary setting or perhaps on a Japanese style terrace, there is beautiful Chinese stoneware; bell shaped pots glazed in the darkest blue with subtle speckled effect. These look superbly understated with crisp white flowers.

A large number of ceramic pots could be a weighty investment, and not just in terms of money. For example, on a roof terrace, you may be better advised to use lightweight plastic containers. These are not so good looking but can be disguised by siting a few lovely handmade pieces at the front of the group. Dense planting will also help to cover them.

Make sure that pots are free draining, allowing 5–10 cm (2–4 in) of broken crocks or pebbles at the base and use a good sterilized loam based compost with vermiculite or a similar product added to lighten it. Never use soil dug from the garden; not only does it contain weed seeds and bugs, but it has the wrong structure for container planting.

A new product available in granular form actually absorbs water and releases it gradually into the soil. Mix this in before planting and save a lot of labour later in watering time; it does not of course mean that you never water again. It makes sense to provide a water tap close to the pots with a hose attached to avoid endless filling and carrying of cans. Computerized watering systems are available too, which link up to tiny mini hoses inserted into each pot; a great boon at holiday time.

Ever in the interest of saving work, incorporate slow release fertilizer granules at the time of planting; this will save hours of mixing up solutions in cans. Alternatively, fertilizers or pesticides can be distributed by means of a dilutor attached to the hose.

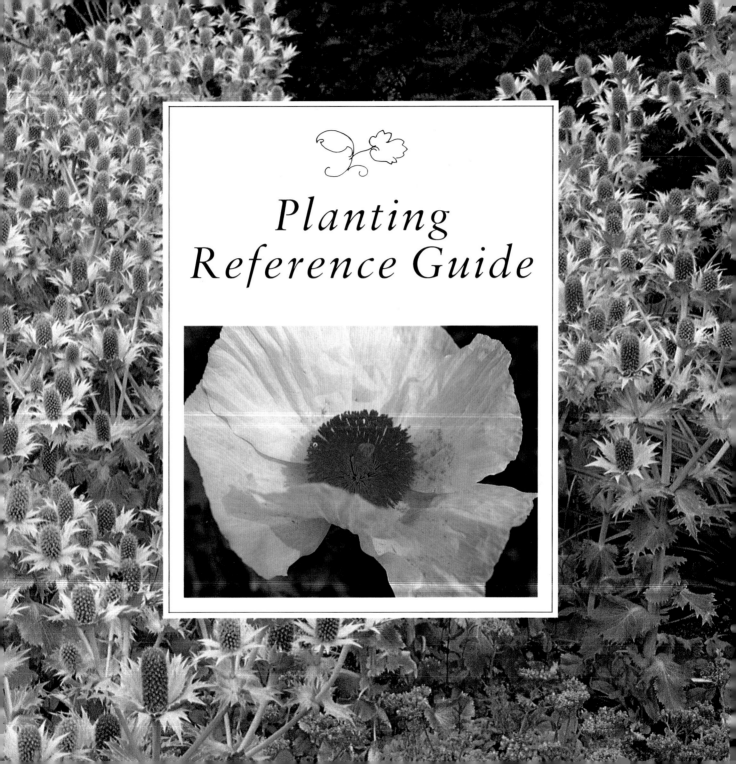

Planting
Reference Guide

Perennial Flowers

Arisaema
A. candidissimum is a charming woodland, tuberous rooted plant with an upright, green-veined, spathe-shaped flower in early summer; H 15 cm (6 in).

Astrantia – Masterwort
Much prized in Elizabethan times, this delightful plant is now regaining popularity. Subtle pinkish green flowers are surrounded by a frilly collar of white papery bracts and grow to a height of 60 cm (2 ft). It has terrific lasting qualities when cut and is lovely in country style flower arrangements. It prefers partial shade and a moist soil.

Astrantia major

Campanula – Bellflower
No garden would be complete without a selection from this large group of plants. Of the taller growing border varieties, try *C. persicifolia* 'Snowdrift', 60–90 cm (2–3 ft) with cup-shaped flowers or *C. latifolia* 'Alba' with larger blooms like long bells borne on tall spikes 1.2–1.5 m (4–5 ft) high. It will do well in sun or semi-shade on any well-drained soil.

Campanula isophylla

Chrysanthemum – Shasta daisy
Making a good show in the border and excellent for cutting, this hardy perennial comes in a variety of flower forms, single, semi-double and double, with blooms up to 10 cm (4 in) across. *C. maximum* 'Wirral Supreme' with large, yellow-centred flowers is one of the best choices.

Cimicifuga – Bugbane
This unusual woodland plant produces tall plumes of flowers and requires plenty of space in a lightly shaded, moist situation, growing to 1.2–1.8 m (4–6 ft) high. *C. foetida* 'White Pearl' is very showy and usefully blooms late in September/October but, as its name implies, is accompanied by an evil smell. *C. racemosa* gives rather more fragrant blooms in July.

Cimicifuga racemosa

Delphinium
These dreamy spires of showy blooms are justifiably prized by every gardener. However they are not easy to grow well and may be best admired when visiting your favourite expertly

tended herbaceous borders during June and July. *D. elatum* 'Butterball' has rich creamy flowers and reaches a height of 1.5–1.8 m (5–6 ft). Easier to cultivate, the Belladonna varieties are smaller (0.9–1.2 m, 3–4 ft), graceful and more branching. 'Moerheimii' is a pure white form. Grow them in fertile soil on a sunny and sheltered site.

Dianthus – Carnation, Pink

The highly perfumed, showy, double-flowered Border carnation, *D. caryophyllus* is well known as a garden and florists' bloom. Old-fashioned pinks like the pure white *D. plumarius* 'Mrs Sinkins' are more delicate in appearance, with slender grey stems and narrow leaves, growing to 30 cm (12 in) high with a single flush of bloom in June. Modern pinks are now tending to be more popular as they are quicker growing with a 'perpetual flowering' habit. Try *D. allwoodii* 'Show Pearl'.

Dicentra eximia alba

Dicentra – Dutchman's breeches

D. spectabilis 'Alba' is a beautiful white form of the popular Bleeding Heart. Graceful arching stems carry pendulous heart-shaped flowers above a clump of feathery grey-green foliage in May and June. Prefers light shade; H 60 cm (2 ft).

Dictamnus – Burning bush

Not to be confused with Kochia, this handsome and strongly aromatic plant truly does burn. The old flower heads are rich in a volatile oil which may be ignited by a match on a warm, still evening to produce a halo of blue flame. *D. albus* carries spikes of spider-like blooms in June/July over glossy, dark leaves; H 60 cm (2 ft).

Eremurus – Foxtail lily

Stately spikes densely covered in scented, starlike flowers rise to a staggering 2.4–3 m (8–10 ft) and, if you have the space to use them, make a good cut bloom. *E. elwesii* 'Albus', flowering in May/June, would make a dramatic spectacle in a large garden. It must have a very sheltered, sunny site to survive, well-drained soil and plenty of water in spring.

Gypsophila – Baby's breath

Billowy clouds of tiny flowers make a perfect foil for the more flamboyant varieties in the border. *G. paniculata* 'Bristol Fairy' with loose panicles of double white blooms from June to August is also most suitable for cutting and drying; H 1 m (3 ft 3 in).

Helleborus – Christmas rose

How welcome are these precious, pure white blooms in the bleak days of winter. The large, saucer-shaped flowers of *H. niger* appear from December to March and will last well, cut for vases. Also evergreen, with thick and spiny greyish foliage, *H. argutifolius* produces interesting greenish flowers in March/April. These both make very useful ground cover plants for the front of a shrub border with partial shade and moist soil; H 60 cm (2 ft).

Paeonia 'Cheddar Gold'

Paeonia – Peony

This large group of perennials contains some of the most magnificent of our garden flowers. The true species of *P. lactiflora* with its scented, pure white blooms has been superseded by numerous hybrids growing up to 1 m (3 ft 3 in) high. These produce single and double, often scented flowers,

10–18 cm (4–7 in) across between late May and July. There are many gorgeous coloured forms, but good white ones include: 'White Wings', sweet smelling, single with yellow centre; 'Festiva Maxima', scented, double with a flush of pink; 'Canarie', double, flushed yellow.

Papaver – Oriental Poppy

Exuberant papery, bowl-shaped flowers up to 15 cm (6 in) across are the excellent reason for growing this otherwise untidy plant. Blooming in June, *P. orientale* 'Perry's White' needs a sunny, well-drained site.

Physostegia – Obedient plant

P. virginiana 'Summer Snow' produces 90 cm (3 ft) spikes of pure white, snapdragon-like flowers from July to September. The blooms will remain in position if pushed to one side, resulting in its strange nickname. It is also easy to grow.

Polygonatum – Solomon's seal

Perfect for a moist woodland or wild garden, *P. × hybridum* produces pendent, green-tipped tubular flowers on arching stems 60–120 cm (2–4 ft) high in May/June. These dangle below pale green leaves making an extremely graceful effect.

Thalictrum – Meadow rue

Often grown for its delicate foliage, reminiscent of the maidenhair fern, *T.*

aquilegifolium 'Album' also offers 15 cm (6 in) long panicles of fluffy white flowers from May to July. It is best planted in drifts to show its light and airy appearance to advantage.

Seasonal Flowers

Campanula – Bellflower

One of the most popular of this large group of useful plants is the Canterbury bell, *C. medium calycanthema* commonly known as the cup and saucer variety because of its large bell-like flowers borne singly along the flower spike from May to July. This hardy biennial grows to 90 cm (3 ft) with a strong upright habit. Even taller is the Chimney bellflower, *C. pyramidalis* with broad spires of white flowers in July.

Chrysanthemum parthenium

Chrysanthemum parthenium – Feverfew

This compact plant produces masses of creamy white cushions of bloom from June to August and is frequently used by herbalists as a relief for migraine. *C.p.* 'Snow Ball' is a good semi-double form and 'Ball's Double White' looks more like tiny tight buttons. H 30 cm (12 in).

Cosmos – Cosmea

A dreamy flower for a glorious late summer show, *C. bipinnatus* floats a show-stopping cloud of single blooms up to 10 cm (4 in) wide across a sea of finely cut, fern-like foliage. It performs best in hot and sunny summers and prefers a light, well-drained soil.

Delphinium – Larkspur

The annual larkspur, *D. consolida* is well worth growing for its densely packed racemes of pure white blooms from June to August. The Giant Imperial strain, reaching a height of 1.2 m (4 ft), is often grown for cutting.

Digitalis – Foxglove

Densely packed with large tubular flowers, these giant spires look sensational in a shady part of the border or in a wild garden. *D. purpurea* is available in shades of white and cream, sometimes flushed with pink or purple, and speckled inside with dark blotches. Flowering in June/July the outstanding 'Excelsior' strain grows to 1.5 m (5 ft) while the 'Shirley Hybrids' which are closer in appearance to the original woodland form, reach a staggering 2.1 m (7 ft).

Digitalis purpurea alba

Dimorphotheca – African daisy
Given a sunny spot and well-drained soil, *D. aurantiaca* 'Glistening White' will produce a continuous show of dazzling, almost silvery, white single daisy blooms from June to September. Though used mainly for bedding it is perennial in milder climates. It is excellent for the front of borders or in tubs and boxes.

D. aurantiaca 'Glistening White'

Hibiscus – Flower of an hour
Most uncommon, this annual *H. trionum* produces large, wide-open creamy flowers with a prominent chocolate-coloured centre. Though each blooms for just one day, they are freely produced from July to September and are well worth trying in a sunny spot; H 45 cm (18 in).

Impatiens – Busy Lizzie
The mainstay bedding plant for shady places, equally at home in tubs and window boxes as it is for underplanting shrubs or providing luxuriant infill amongst perennials. The flat, single blooms have petals which seem to glow with luminosity, brightening the most unpromising location. Its only special need is moist soil.

Lathyrus – Sweet pea
This easily grown climber, *L. odoratus*, with its delicately scented flowers is ideal for covering a trellis or pergola. Perfect, too, for flower arrangements, as the more they are cut, the more they bloom. The Spencer variety, 'White Ensign' will produce good perfume and showy blooms. Give them a sunny site and a deep planting hole with plenty of organic matter incorporated. H 3 m (10 ft).

Lobelia
Known most commonly as a blue bedding plant, the variety *L. erinus* 'White Gem' is worth considering for window boxes with *L. erinus pendula*, a pretty trailing form for hanging baskets. H 25 cm (10 in).

Lunaria – Honesty
Although the flowers of *L. annua* 'Alba' are not particularly spectacular, this plant comes into its own in late summer when it produces lovely flat seed pods with the appearance of mother-of-pearl. These are eminently suitable for drying for winter flower arrangements. H 45 cm (18 in).

Matthiola – Stocks
Perfect for bedding or for cottage gardens, these highly fragrant flowers grow in dense clusters on spikes from 30–60 cm (1–2 ft) high. *M. incana* 'Ten Week Stock' is a half-hardy annual blooming in midsummer,

while the denser 'Brompton Stock' appears earlier in the season. They need well-drained soil in sun or light shade.

Moluccella – Bells of Ireland

Not actually a white flower, but very valuable nevertheless for its tall spikes of unusual lime green 'flowers' which are actually a bell-shaped calyx surrounding an insignificant white bloom. *M. laevis* grows to a height of 60 cm (2 ft) flowers in late summer and is good for cutting and drying by the glycerine method. Well-drained soil, sun or light shade is required.

Nicotiana affinis

Nicotiana – Tobacco plant

A much loved plant with a wonderful evening fragrance, *N. affinis* grows up to 90 cm (3 ft) high with clusters of pure white tubular flowers which open mainly at the end of the day. Modern compact varieties such as 'Dwarf White Bedder' flower throughout the summer, all day long, and 'Lime Green' makes a terrific splash of 'non-colour' in the garden and is superb for flower arrangements. This plant is very easy to grow and tolerates shady situations, making it an ideal choice in town.

Pelargonium – Geranium

One of the most enduring and popular summer flowers for boxes, tubs and hanging baskets, it exists in many forms, leaf colours and habits. The two most useful are *P. hortorum hybrid*, the Zonal Pelargonium (H 30–60 cm, 1–2 ft), with an upright bushy habit and the fleshy-leaved, trailing ivy-leaved type, *P. peltatum hybrid* (H 60–90 cm, 2–3 ft). 'Queen of the Whites' is a good Zonal and 'Elégante' is a delightful trailer with pink-flushed, white blooms and white-edged leaves which turn purple as the season progresses. Pelargoniums/geraniums do best in full sun, planted in a sandy loam.

Petunia

Another good tub plant for a sunny site, the showy funnel-shaped flowers of *P. hybrida* repeat flower all summer as long as they are regularly dead-headed and fed with a high potash fertilizer. H 30 cm (12 in).

Viola – Pansy

Modern garden pansies, *V. × wittrockiana* are now available in both winter- and summer-flowering varieties. Low-growing, spreading plants, they have charming, wide-open blooms. 'Ice King' and 'White Swan' are good whites. Grow pansies in moist, well-drained soil in sun or part shade. H 15 cm (6 in).

Bulbs

Cardiocrinum – Giant Himalayan lily

For a dramatic statement, *C. giganteum* will produce up to twenty fragrant, creamy, trumpet-shaped blooms, 15 cm (6 in) long on a 2.7 m (9 ft) stem. Bulbs die after flowering so they need to be replanted each autumn in a position with well-drained, moisture-retentive soil and light shade. They bloom in midsummer.

Convallaria – Lily of the valley

Always a welcome sight in early spring, these tiny, fragrant blooms dangling from curved stems, peep out from dark green, lance-shaped leaves. *C. majalis* spreads by creeping rhizomes and should be planted during the winter months in a shady position with moist soil.

Crinum

Clusters of large lily-like flowers appear on 60 cm (2 ft) stems, surrounded by elegant strap-like leaves in late summer. This beautiful plant has only one drawback; it is rather tender and must be grown in a warm, sunny and sheltered position with well-drained but moisture-retentive soil. Plant in spring.

Crocus

Essential for the spring garden or rockery, C. *vernus* 'Joan of Arc' shows off its large cup-shaped blooms to advantage if planted in large drifts; H 15 cm (6 in). The species C. *chrysanthus* 'Snow Bunting' with its deep yellow centres and the lovely star-shaped flowers of C. *biflorus weldenii* both appear in spring while the autumn flowering C. *speciosus aitchisonii* 'Alba' is well worth considering. Plant the corms in autumn in well-drained soil with sun or part shade. They may be naturalized in lawns or under deciduous trees.

Crocus

Erythronium – Dog's-tooth violet

For a woodland or spring garden, E. *dens-canis* 'White Splendour' produces nodding heads of delicate blooms 15 cm (6 in) high, from clumps of dark reddish leaves blotched with green. The form E. *revolutum* 'White Beauty' grows to 30 cm (12 in) and is quite stunning with its pure white, yellow-centred flowers set off by mottled foliage. Plant the tubers in autumn in a shady site with moist soil.

Galanthus – Snowdrop

The herald of the New Year, snowdrops look best planted in clumps to show off their tiny, nodding, green tipped blooms. G. *nivalis* 'S. Arnott' growing to 25 cm (10 in) has larger flowers than the species. Plant bulbs in autumn in moist soil with light shade.

Galtonia – Summer hyacinth

A rather surprising kind of hyacinth, G. *candicans* blooms in late summer on stalks up to 1.2 m (4 ft) high. Not as fragrant as the true *Hyacinthus orientalis*, but nevertheless interesting for a border. Plants the bulbs 20 cm (8 in) deep in spring and choose a sunny site.

Hyacinthus – Hyacinth

Dense clusters of highly perfumed, pure white, bell-shaped flowers clothe the 22 cm (9 in) stems of H. *orientalis* 'L'Innocence'. This is an ideal bulb for planting in tubs or window boxes as it gives a tremendous show but does not

generally naturalize well in the garden. In any case, the bulbs should be lifted and stored after the leaves die down and replanted in the following autumn, though flowers in the next year will be much smaller. Give extra peat for moisture when planting.

Lilium 'Sterling Star'

Lilium – Lily

These sumptuous waxy, trumpet-shaped flowers with their heady perfume evoke such wonderful images of grandeur and luxury that it hardly seems possible that they can just emerge from the ground. There are very many varieties of all hues including pure whites, rich creams, pink flushed and some with yellow stripes and speckles. These are some of the best: *L. candidum* (Madonna lily), pure white, H 1.2–1.5 m (4–5 ft); *L. longiflorum* (Easter lily), pure white, H 90 cm (3 ft), good for pot culture; *L. regale*, white with yellow centre, outside of petals shaded rose-purple, H 1.5 m (5 ft); *L.* Imperial Gold, very large, wide-open, pure white blooms with a strong band of gold on each petal and heavy crimson spotting, H 1.5–2.1 m (5–7 ft). All these are heavily fragrant. Lilies require very well-drained soil and a sunny site. Many are suitable for growing in pots out of doors or in the greenhouse.

Narcissus – Daffodil

This large family of bulbs contains subjects to flower right through the spring season with a wide variety of forms and heights. They should be planted in autumn in a sunny or partly shaded position. These are some of the best whites.

Trumpet form, H 30–45 cm (12–18 in): *N.* 'Trousseau', white petals, yellow trumpet; 'Beersheeba', pure white; 'Mount Hood', white petals, creamy trumpet.

Large-cupped form, H 35–45 cm (14–18 in): *N.* 'Ice Follies', white petals, yellow cup; 'Tenedos', cream petals, cup deeper tone.

Small-cupped form, H 35–45 cm (14–18 in): 'La Riante', pure white

petals, bright orange cup; 'Chinese White' and 'Polar Ice', both all white.

Double form, H 30–45 cm (12–18 in), one to three flowers per stem: 'Irene Copeland', white/yellow interspersed petals; 'Cheerfulness', creamy double, late flowering.

Triandrus form, H 20–40 cm (8–16 in), pendent flowers, swept back petals: 'Thalia', pale cream; 'Rippling Waters', pure white.

Poeticus form, H 35–45 cm (14–18 in): 'Cantabile', pure white petals, green cup with red edge.

Narcissus 'Actaea'

Trillium – Wake robin

A delightful woodland plant needing shade from trees above and plenty of leaf mould in the ground. All parts of the plant are arranged in threes; 3 broad leaves, 3 green sepals and 3 large petals, growing up to 45 cm (18 in) and flowering in spring. *T. grandiflorum* is pure white, fading to pink, while *T. undulatum* has purple streaks in its petals.

Tulipa – Tulip

A well-loved large family of flowering bulbs composed of many flower forms which are invaluable for spring bedding schemes. Plant late in the year in well-drained soil with a sunny situation. 'Diana', single early white; 'Schoonoord', double early white; 'Athleet', Mendel white; 'Pax', Triumph white; 'White Triumphator', lily-flowered; 'Zwanenburg', Darwin hybrid.

Tulipa batalinii

Flowering Shrubs

Abelia

This attractive, slow-growing bush is covered in scented, white and pink-flushed tubular blooms from mid-summer to autumn. *A.* × *grandiflora* 'Copper Glow' has small bronze-green, glossy leaves and will remain semi-evergreen in a sheltered site. It needs protection from wind and thrives best in full sun. H 1.5–1.8 m (5–6 ft) × S 0.9–1.2 m (3–4 ft).

Abeliophyllum – White forsythia

Though rather untidy, *A. distichum* is well worth growing for its white version of forsythia blooms, appearing in winter when little else is in flower. It is vigorous and quite hardy but should be positioned at the back of a border behind some more elegant plants to disguise it during the rest of the year. H 1.8 m (6 ft).

Amelanchier – Snowy mespilus

These versatile shrubs can stand alone as a feature in the garden or be integrated into a mixed border. *A. canadensis* gives interest for most of the year, commencing with masses of tiny, white starry flowers which appear before coppery tinged leaves in early spring. Edible black fruits follow in summer with a splendid show of brilliant orange-red foliage to complete the cycle in autumn. 'Ballerina' is a larger flowered form. Best in a sunny site. H and S 3 m (10 ft).

Buddleia – Butterfly bush

A fast-growing shrub producing dense plumes of fragrant, pure white flowers at the end of long arching stems right through the summer. *B. davidii* 'White Profusion' and 'White Cloud' are good forms. Its very special characteristic is its attraction to butterflies with which it will often be covered when in flower. It prefers sun and will tolerate most soils. Cut back hard in spring. H and S 2.7 m (9 ft).

Carpenteria

C. californica is an excellent evergreen shrub of densely bushy habit. In early summer it is covered with brilliant white, single, anemone-shaped flowers with a delightful scent. Though tolerant of most soils, it is rather tender so must be sited where it will be protected from cold and harsh winds H 3 m (10 ft) × S 1.8–2.4 m (6–8 ft).

Carpenteria californica

Choisya – Mexican orange

Another handsome evergreen bush; *C. ternata* earns its name from its glossy, dark green foliage, aromatic when crushed, and the masses of fragrant, waxy flowers which cover the plant during spring and early summer. A good feature specimen, it needs well-drained soil, sunshine and the protection of a south wall in cooler climates. H 1.8 m (6 ft) × S 1.8–2.4 m (6–8 ft).

Cistus – Rock rose

These are sun-loving plants which continuously produce brilliant saucer-like flowers with the texture of crumpled tissue paper in early summer. *Cistus × aguilari*, H and S 1.2–1.5 m (4–5 ft), is pure white with yellow stamens and *C. ladanifer*, H 1.8 m (6 ft) × S 1.2 m (4 ft), is distinguished by prominent purplish blotches at the base of each petal. *C. × corbariensis* is one of the hardiest, with freely borne blooms with a yellow splash on white petals; it is low and spreading, H 0.9–1.2 m (3–4 ft) × S 1.8–2.7 m (6–9 ft). Good for hot, dry banks and will tolerate seaside situations.

Deutzia

One of the prettiest pure white forms of these attractive deciduous shrubs is *D. gracilis*, making panicles of starry flowers in early summer, H 0.9–1.2 m (3–4 ft) × S 1.2–1.8 m (4–6 ft). For a stronger statement, choose *D. × magnifica* with panicles of double, pompom-like blooms, H 2.4 m (8 ft) × S 1.8–2.4 m (6–8 ft), or *D. scabra* 'Candidissima' with double, cup-shaped flowers, H 1.8–3 m (6–10 ft) × S 1.2–1.8 m (4–6 ft). Best in full sun with light shelter.

Deutzia setchuenensis corymbiflora

Eucryphia

These are beautiful small trees of columnar form, which are so slow growing that they can easily take their place in the shrub border. During summer and autumn they are literally smothered in large saucer shaped blooms with a prominent boss of yellow stamens. *E. glutinosa*, attaining a height of 3 m (10 ft), is partially evergreen and the hardiest of the species. *E. × nymansensis* is a quicker growing evergreen reaching 4.5 m (15 ft) and hardy in milder regions. Soil should be moist and cool but they flower best in a sunny situation.

Gaultheria

G. procumbens is a useful evergreen ground covering shrub spreading to 90 cm (3 ft) but with a height of only about 15 cm (6 in). Small white flowers in late summer are followed by red fruits. *G. cuneata* is similar but with white fruits. Moist, acid soil is required.

Hebe – Veronica

These small evergreen shrubs are suitable for a mixed border or for seasonal display in tubs or window boxes. *H. albicans*, H and S 60 cm (2 ft), is covered in spikes of tiny white flowers in mid summer.

Helianthemum – Rock rose

An excellent small shrub for a grey foliage scheme, *H. nummularium* 'The Bride' is smothered in single blooms, white with a yellow centre, during summer. Growing to 15 cm (6 in) and spreading to 60 cm (2 ft), this is best sited on a sunny bank with free draining soil.

Hibiscus – Tree hollyhock

A very showy member of the mallow family, giving late summer/early autumn display, *H. syriacus* produces a succession of dramatic but short lived flowers. There are several white varieties: 'Jeanne d'Arc' is a compact, double form; 'Dorothy Crane' is a pure white single with a crimson centre; 'Elegantissimus' is double with a maroon centre. Choose a sunny site with well drained soil. H to 3 m (10 ft) × S 1.2 –1.8 m (4–6ft).

Hibiscus syriacus 'Totus Albus'

Hydrangea

This large family of late flowering deciduous shrubs contains some of our favourite garden plants. The showy inflorescences composed of sterile and fertile florets are most familiar in the mophead (Hortensia) form, *H. macro-*

phylla. However, the Lacecap form, 'Lanarth White' is lovely with its circle of pure white florets surrounding a flat cap of tiny pale blue or pink flowers. Most spectacular is *H. paniculata* 'Grandiflora' with its huge panicles of creamy white blooms at the ends of graceful, arching stems. Hydrangeas must have deep, moist soil with plenty of water in summer. H 2.4–3 m (8–10 ft) × S 1.2–1.8 m (4–6ft).

Magnolia × soulangeana

Magnolia
Every white garden should find a place for at least one variety of these magnificent plants. The evergreen *M. grandiflora* is a superb wall shrub with its huge, glossy leaves and complementary waxy, cream, scented flowers appearing in late summer; H 3–4.5 m (10–15 ft) × S 1.8–3 m (6–10 ft). *M. × soulangeana* produces glorious white blooms with purplish staining at the base on bare stems before the leaves appear in spring. Growing to a height

and spread of 3–4.5 m (10–15 ft), this makes a good specimen tree for a large space. In a smaller garden, *M. stellata* is charming, covered with starry, scented white flowers in early spring. H and S 2.4–3 m (8–10 ft). Grow magnolias in a site sheltered from north and east winds.

Malus – Crab apple
An attractive specimen tree for spring and autumn show; *M.* 'Lady Northcliffe' is smothered in early white blossom, with good yellow fruit later in the year. H 3.6–4.5 m (12–15 ft).

Osmanthus
Of this attractive group of evergreen, white flowering shrubs, *O. delavayi* gives the best show. It is covered in tiny, scented, tubular flowers in early spring and grows to a height and spread of 1.8–2.4 m (6–8 ft). It does best in a sheltered site.

Paeonia
The shrubby tree peony, *P. suffruticosa* makes a handsome foliage plant with huge, though short lived, flowers in early summer. 'Rock's Variety' has white, single blooms with dark crimson blotches at the base of the petals and prominent yellow stamens. H to 2.4 m (8 ft).

Philadelphus – Mock orange
This is one of the loveliest of the summer flowering white shrubs pro-

ducing masses of single or double blooms with a delicious scent. There are many to choose from; *P.* 'Virginal' is a double form appearing in pendent clusters, H 3 m (10 ft); 'Belle Etoile' is a large flowered single with a dark pink centre and strongly fragrant, H 3 m (10 ft). Plant in full sun.

Philadelphus coronarius

Prunus – Ornamental cherry
No spring garden would be complete without cherry blossom. The pure white virginal freshness of *P.* 'Shirotae' with its clusters of scented, double formed flowers set off by dark and glossy bark is an uplifting sight after a long, gloomy winter. 'Tai Haku' has

larger, single blossoms and beautiful bronzy foliage. *P. subhirtella* 'Autumnalis' is distinguished by semi-double white flowers appearing throughout the winter. These trees grow to a height of 4.5 –6 m (15–20 ft), are shallow rooted and unfussy about soil.

Rhododendron

These are some of the loveliest of the spring-flowering shrubs with their enormous clusters of bell-shaped blooms, often delicately speckled with darker tones and with long thin stamens with the appearance of tiny jewels. H 0.9–4.5 m (3–15 ft). White flowering evergreen forms include *R.* 'Avalanche' with cascades of pure white with orange stamens, *R. calophytum* with long, narrow leaves, *R. fictolacteum* with dark red blotches and 'Penjerrick Cream', primrose opening to ivory. This is an enormous group of plants which also includes the Japanese azaleas; sizes and habits vary but they all require an acid soil, moisture and a sheltered situation.

Romneya – Tree poppy

R. coulteri is a vigorous sub-shrub making a dense bush of greyish green leaves. In late summer, numerous fragrant large, flat flowers with tissue-paper petals and deep yellow centres are produced. Plant in light soil with a sunny aspect and do not move as they resent root disturbance. H 1.8–2.4 m (6–8 ft).

Spiraea – Bridal wreath

The spring flowering *S. × arguta* is smothered in arching spires of tiny white flowers. This deciduous shrub, growing to a height and spread of 1.8 m (6 ft), makes a delightfully frothy show in the border.

Syringa – Lilac

Though most familiar as a wonderfully scented mauve flowering tree, the lilac produces some lovely white forms. *S. vulgaris* (common lilac) is a large upright shrub with pyramidal panicles of blooms in late spring. 'Candeur' has large creamy flowers, 'Maud Notcutt' is vigorous with dominant panicles of single blooms and 'Madame Lemoine' is an excellent double form. A very undemanding shrub; site it near a path to enjoy the perfume. H 2.4–3 m (8–10 ft) × S 1.8 m (6 ft).

Viburnum

This is a very large genus of white flowering shrubs, frequently sweetly scented, often giving autumn colour and some blooming in winter. Many will take a shady aspect and the winter flowering varieties are particularly useful. *V. × bodnantense* is deciduous with a stiff habit, is frost resistant and its pink flushed clusters of flowers appear in mid-winter on bare stems; H 2.7–3.6 m (9–12 ft). *V. × carlcephalum* is deciduous with broad heads of creamy, fragrant flowers in

Viburnum plicatum 'Mariesii'

spring; H 2.1 m (7 ft). *V. carlesii* of a more compact, bushy habit is deciduous and in spring produces masses of heads of very fragrant waxy blooms. *V. opulus* 'Sterile' (snowball bush) produces huge, round flower heads on a tall, deciduous bush; H 4.5 m (15 ft) × S 3.6–4.5 m (12–15 ft). *V. tinus* 'French White' is a glossy evergreen flowering through winter to spring; H 2.1 m (7 ft). *V. plicatum* 'Mariesii' resembles a wedding cake with its tiered branches literally smothered in wide, flat lacecap flowers in spring; deciduous, H 2.4–3 m (8–10ft) × S 3–4.5 m (10–15 ft).

Old Cottage Garden Roses

Shrubs

'Blanche Fleur'; a famous Centifolia with stongly perfumed, medium-sized flowers with a faint blush. Early and profuse flowering, good for pot-pourri. H 1.2 m (4 ft) × S 0.9 m (3 ft).

'Alba Maxima'; very full, strongly fragrant flowers, pinkish in bud and opening to rich white. H 1.8 m (6 ft) × S 1.5 m (5 ft) as a shrub or can climb to 3.6 m (12 ft).

'Madame Plantier'; an Alba hybrid with pale greyish foliage of almost thornless stems. The pure white, very double flowers are richly perfumed and good for pot-pourri. Similar to the lesser known 'La Virginale'. H 1.8 (6 ft) × S 1.2 m (4 ft); or, as a climber H 3 m (10 ft).

'Boule de Neige'; a Bourbon with small, reflexed flowers growing in groups of three, repeat flowering. The fine fragrance is a combination of the Damask and Tea roses. H 1.2 m (4 ft) × S 0.9 m (3 ft).

'Blanc Double de Coubert'; a Rugosa which is typically tough and good for poor conditions. Produces semi-double, ivory-white flowers throughout summer. Very vigorous and reliable. H 1.8 m (6 ft) × S 1.5 m (5 ft).

Rosa 'Souvenir de la Malmaison'

Rosa Dupontii'; strongly growing with musk scented, large, semi-double flowers and grey-green foliage. H 1.8 m (6 ft) × S 1.8 m (6 ft).

Rosa spinosissima 'Double Cream'; prolific flowering with cream blooms and golden stamens. Greyish leaves produced on dark red stems. Most unusual, stylish black fruits in autumn.

Climbers

'Aimée Vibert'; a Noisette with pure white, small double blooms produced in large clusters throughout summer. Attractive, shiny foliage good for arbours and arches but slow to establish. H 4.5 m (15 ft).

'Mme. Alfred Carrière'; a hardy and trouble-free Noisette producing well-scented, clear white flowers throughout summer. Good for a north wall. H 7.5 m (25 ft).

Ramblers

'Alberic Barbier'; a reliable Wichuriana with large, creamy, fragrant flowers which are yellow in bud and produced in small clusters. Strong growing and good for a north wall. H 7.5 m (25 ft).

'Bobby James'; a powerful grower reaching 9 m (30 ft) with large trusses of fragrant, single flowers. Good for large walls or over trees.

'Félicité et Perpétue; a thick-growing Sempervirens with small but full, delicately scented, creamy flowers

in large clusters. Late flowering with one crop. H 6 m (20 ft).

'Rambling Rector'; profusely flowering rambler 6 m (20 ft) high, with large clusters of musk-scented, small, creamy blooms.

Rosa 'Bobbie James'

Wall & Pergola

Abutilon

A. vitifolium 'Album' is a near-hardy species suitable for growing as a wall shrub, freely producing its large single flowers from early summer until autumn. Needs full sun, shelter and well drained soil. H 2.4 m (8 ft).

Clematis

This is an enormous family of large and small flowered climbers, both evergreen and deciduous, suitable for covering arbours, walls, trellises and pergolas. Clematis must have deep, rich, cool soil for its roots but generally flowers best in full sun.

C. armandii, a vigorous glossy

evergreen which in spring is covered with white saucer shaped flowers. *C.a.* 'Snowdrift' has larger pure white flowers. Both need a sheltered, sunny site; good for pergolas, H 9 m (30 ft) × S 7.5–18 m (25–60 ft).

C. calycina and *C. cirrhosa* are both small flowered hardy evergreens blooming in winter.

C. fosterii is a most uncommon, lemon-scented species suitable for a cold conservatory.

C. flammula is covered in masses of small scented flowers in late summer, good for growing through trees or spring flowering shrubs.

C. florida alba plena has large, greenish flowers with a huge mound of green stamens in the centre; *C.f. bicolour* is beautiful and unusual, with creamy flowers with a prominent mound of purple stamens but must be grown in a very sheltered position outside or in a cold greenhouse.

C. montana 'Alba' is an extremely vigorous, deciduous spring flowering form. Literally smothered with small, pure white flowers for up to two months and wonderful for covering a large space or an ugly wall; H 12 m (40 ft) × S 4.5–6 m (15–20 ft). *C.m.* 'Alexander' has scented creamy blooms and *C.m.* 'Wilsonii' is similar but smelling of hot chocolate.

C. recta, a herbaceous perennial, makes a bush of tiny white flowers.

C. spooneri is similar to montana, but with larger blooms, very vigorous

Clematis montana 'Spooneri'

Clematis 'Marie Boisselot'

and free flowering.

Of the large flowered summer hybrids choose from 'Duchess of Edinburgh' with early double blooms followed by a flush of single flowers in autumn, the exceedingly vigorous and free flowering 'Marie Boisselot' with pure white blooms up to 15 cm (6 in) across, or 'Henryi', elegant single, purest white with yellow tipped, white stamens. The white 'Snow Queen' and pearly-grey 'Silver Moon' are both good for a north wall.

Chaenomeles – Japanese quince

C. speciosa 'Apple Blossom' is an attractive white form of this popular shrub. Its spring flowers are followed in autumn by fragrant, edible, green-yellow fruits. Best trained against a wall in a sunny spot, H and S to 1.8 m (6 ft).

Cobaea – Cup and saucer vine

C. scandens 'Alba' is a useful quick growing annual producing unusual green and white flowers from mid-summer and into winter. Good for filling in spaces while slower to establish climbers are growing. H to 6 m (20 ft).

Hydrangea

H. petiolaris is a hardy, deciduous climbing species which attaches itself to the wall by means of suckers. Flat corymbs of creamy flowers, up to 25 cm (10 in) across, are produced in early summer. H to 18 m (60 ft).

Jasminum – Jasmine

J. officinale is hardy and vigorous, making a tangled mass of twining stems and ferny leaves, smothered in tiny, highly scented white blooms throughout the summer. Best in well-drained soil and a sunny situation. Deciduous; cut back hard in winter.

J. polyanthum is less hardy with pink flushed flowers, semi-evergreen, H 3 m (10 ft); also suitable for a cool conservatory.

Lonicera – Honeysuckle

A favourite family of perfumed climbing shrubs suitable for covering walls, trellis and pergolas. Plant in deep, rich soil in a position with some light shade.

L. fragrantissima, 1.8 m (6 ft), is evergreen with highly fragrant, cream flowers produced in winter.

L. japonica (Japanese) is a vigorous evergreen making a tangled mass of growth up to 9 m (30 ft), with fragrant white and yellow flowers in summer.

L. periclymenum 'Belgica' (early Dutch) and 'Serotina' (late Dutch) produce creamy flowers flushed with purple and pink, early and late in summer, respectively. H 4.5–6 m (15–20 ft).

L. × purpusii, H 1.8 m (6 ft), is deciduous with scented, creamy flowers in winter.

Passiflora – Passion flower

P. caerulea 'Constance Elliot' is a pure white and hardy form of this interesting and exotic-looking climber. Best grown on a south wall for protection.

Polygonum – Russian vine

P. baldschuanicum is a rampant climber which becomes smothered in panicles of tiny, white flowers in late summer. Can grow 3 –4.5 m (10–15 ft) a year, eventually reaching 12 m (40 ft). Marvellous for covering a large, ugly area or for climbing through old trees; a good, instant screen.

Pyracantha – Firethorn

A group of hardy, evergreen wall shrubs with winter fruits and white flowers in summer. Full sun or part shade; train and support on wires.

P. atalantioides 'Aurea', of upright habit, H 3–4.5 m (10–15 ft), is fast growing with bright yellow berries.

P. crenulata rogersiana is a spreading form, H 2.4 m (8 ft) × S 4.5 m (15 ft), with orange-red fruits while those of *P.c.* 'Flava' are yellow.

Solanum jasminoides 'Album'

Solanum

S. jasminoides 'Album' is a delightfully delicate looking member of the potato family, producing tiny starlike flowers from mid-summer to autumn. Only for sheltered areas or a cold conservatory. H 3–4.5 m (10–15 ft).

Trachelospermum

Evergreen climbing, twining shrubs needing support, for a sheltered, sunny wall and light, acid soil. Sweetly fragrant, tiny white flowers are freely produced in late summer.

T. asiaticum, dense and compact to 4.5 m (15 ft).

T. jasminoides, 3.6 m (12 ft), also suitable for a cool conservatory.

T.j. 'Variegatum' has leaves mottled and edged with white.

T. majus is more vigorous, growing to 6 m (20 ft), but not so fragrant.

Wisteria

One of the most beautiful climbing shrubs, producing large, drooping racemes of flowers in spring. Though slow to establish, it is suitable for walls, arches and pergolas. Best with a south or west aspect. Prune back all growths to within three buds of the previous year's growth in February.

W. floribunda 'Alba', vigorous to 9 m (30 ft), with fragrant flowers.

W. sinensis 'Alba', the most popular form, grows to 30 m (100 ft) with dense racemes of fragrant flowers up to 30 cm (12 in) long.

W. venusta produces 10–15 cm (4–6 in) racemes of scented flowers and reaches a height of 9 m (30 ft).

Permanent Framework

Buxus – Box

B. sempervirens is a slow-growing shrub up to 3 m (10 ft) with small rounded, glossy leaves suitable for sun or semi-shade. It is a classic for topiary work and hedging. *B. s.* 'Suffruticosa' is a dwarf form for edging and knot gardens while 'Latifolia Maculata' makes a compact bush with broad leaves marked with yellow.

Buxus sempervirens

× *Cupressocyparis* – Leyland cypress

A fast growing hybrid conifer, × C. *leylandii* is happy on any ordinary soil. Of conical form, with a possible height of 15 m (50 ft), it can be used to make a dense hedge, clipped into slabs and arches for screening ugly views or as a wind break. Plant 45–60 cm (18–24 in) apart and stop main growing shoot when it reaches the desired height.

'Leighton Green' is cone bearing and rich green, 'Haggerston Grey' is more glaucous.

Fatsia – Castor oil plant

Fatsia japonica has dramatic, dark green foliage formed like giant hands, surmounted in autumn by globes of tiny white flowers in 45 cm (18 in) branched panicles. Needs shelter from wind but its tolerance of shade makes it an excellent courtyard plant. Height and spread to 4.5 m (15 ft).

Hedera – Ivy

An enormous family of self-clinging climbers useful for evergreen cover of walls and stonework or as ground cover. Dark green types such as *H. helix* (English ivy) survive in dense shade, while variegated forms need good light. *H. canariensis* 'Gloire de Marengo' is a rapidly growing, large-leaved form with grey-green and white markings.

Ilex – Holly

A large group of slow-growing, prickly leaved evergreen trees and shrubs which bear bright red berries in winter when male and female plants are grown together. Variegated forms need sun to produce good colour. *I. aquifolium* 'Silver Queen' has white margins with pink growth in spring, 'Aurea-marginata' is yellow edged and 'Bacciflava' produces yellow berries with all green leaves.

Laurus – Sweet bay

A Mediterranean shrub with aromatic leaves used in cooking. It can be damaged by cold winds and is vulnerable to pest attack by leaf scale and aphid. In open ground *L. nobilis* can reach a height of 5.4 m (18 ft) but is more usually grown in tubs trained into forms of pyramids, balls or standards. These are best used formally in pairs or rows in the Italian manner.

Ligustrum – Privet

These hardy evergreen shrubs can be quickly established as a hedge by setting young plants 30–45 cm (12–18 in) apart. *L. ovalifolium* can grow to 4.5 m (15 ft) with oval, mid-green foliage and scented white flowers like miniature lilac appearing in July. *L.o.* 'Aureum' (Golden privet) has yellow leaves, splashed green in the centre, 'Variegatum' has pale, almost cream edging.

Lonicera nitida 'Baggesen's Gold'

Lonicera

L. nitida is a relative of the honeysuckle, but quite unlike it in habit. Tiny ovate glossy, dark green leaves are arranged neatly on either side of the stems, making a dense, compact shrub 1.5 m (5 ft) round. It tolerates shade and is excellent for hedging and topiary. 'Baggesen's Gold' is a brilliant yellow form needing sun to maintain its colour.

Magnolia – Laurel magnolia
Spectacular evergreen tree on a grand scale, best grown as a fine wall shrub. Its leaves are lustrous dark green with felted rust coloured undersides, 25 cm (10 in) long. Huge, fragrant creamy flowers are produced from July to September. Not suitable for cold areas. H 4.5 m (15 ft) or more.

Phormium – New Zealand flax
A slightly tender sub-shrub producing sword-shaped leaves fanning out from the base to form striking, vigorous clumps, excellent as a dramatic feature plant. *P. tenax* is slightly tender, requiring moist soil and full sun; to 2.7 m (9 ft). Glaucous green is the usual colour but 'Atropurpureum' is bronze and 'Variegatum' is striped green and yellow.

Rosmarinus – Rosemary
Sun-loving aromatic shrub with needle-like leaves used in cooking. As a hedge, it gives a buoyant and vigorous effect up to 1.8 m (6 ft) high. *R. officinalis* 'Miss Jessop's Upright' has particularly vertical lines and makes

pale mauve flowers in March. 'Albiflorus' is an unusual white-flowered form. Needs well-drained soil.

Rosmarinus officinalis

Taxus – Common yew
T. baccata is an evergreen conifer bearing brilliant red poisonous berries. Remarkably tolerant and surviving to a great age, it is slow growing eventually reaching a height and breadth of 4.5 m (15 ft). Its dense, dark green needles make this the best conifer for architectural hedging and detailed topiary work.

Foliage Effect

Acanthus – Bear's breeches
Herbaceous perennials with extremely handsome foliage and tall flowering spikes needing deep, well-drained soil and sun. *A. mollis latifolius* has mid-green leaves with wavy margins and 45 cm (18 in) spikes of white and purple flowers in summer; it will tolerate some shade, H 90 cm (3 ft). *A. spinosus* has darker, spiny and deeply-cut foliage with similar flowers, H 0.9–1.2 m (3–4 ft).

Acanthus mollis

Alchemilla

A. mollis makes a delightful foliage perennial, forming clumps of hairy, pale green leaves which glisten with water droplets after rain. Feathery branches of lime-green flowers cover the plant throughout summer, H 45 cm (18 in). Needs moist, well-drained soil and sun or part shade.

Angelica

A. archangelica is a short-lived perennial herb which is well worth growing for its architectural, deeply incised, light green leaves. Tall clusters of yellow-green flowers appear in late summer. It needs moist soil and sun. H 1.8–3 m (6–10 ft).

Arundinaria fastuosa

Arundinaria – Bamboo

A large group of hardy, evergreen bamboos, some of which can be very invasive. They are useful for background effects in water gardens or formal Japanese style designs. *A. muriela* is clump forming with rigid stems and dark green leaves, H 1.8–2.4 cm (6–8 ft). *A. nitida* is fast growing and needs space; stems are purple with bright green leaves, shade tolerant, H 2.7–3 m (10 ft). *A. variegata* forms dense thickets of dark green zig-zagged canes with white-striped, mid-green leaves. H 1.2 m (4 ft). They need moist soil, sun and shelter from winds.

Astilbe

A. rivularis is a large growing form of the species, with very striking leaves and arching stems of greenish-flowers. Although it can grow to a height of 1.8 m (6 ft) the effect it gives is light and airy next to denser large plants. A hardy perennial needing moist soil.

Cordyline – Cabbage palm

Cordylines have an exotic, palm-like appearance, making good specimens for a garden with a Meditteranean feel. They associate well with grey and silver plants. *C. australis* is a slow-growing form with strap-shaped grey-green leaves borne in clusters at the top of branching stems, up to 7.5 m (25 ft) high. *C. indivisa* is more common as a pot plant for the terrace

when it will grow to 1.2 m (4 ft). They need well-drained soil and sun, and are usefully tolerant of seaside winds.

Cornus – Dogwood

C. alba is a deciduous, suckering shrub with good variegated forms, often with bright red stems in winter. *C.a.* 'Spaethii' has golden variegated leaves and red winter bark, 'Westonbirt' produces exceptionally brilliant red stems. *C. stolonifera* 'Flaviramea' has interesting bright yellow-green winter stems. Cut back to ground level in late winter to promote fresh, new growth in spring.

Euphorbia

A large group of perennials and sub-shrubs with striking, architectural forms, needing sun and well-drained soil. *E. characias* has blue-grey oblong leaves along spikes topped with clusters of sulphur yellow inflorescences in early summer, and measures 0.9–1.2 m (3–4 ft). *E. wulfenii* makes a bushy sub-shrub with narrow blue-green leaves and bright yellow-green flower bracts arranged in 23 cm (9 in) terminal panicles, and also racemes 1.2 m (4 ft).

Gunnera

The giant of the garden, *G. manicata* produces dramatic dark-green, toothed and spiny leaves up to 3 m (10 ft) across on equally spiny stems. Tall cones of green flowers develop through the summer. Must have deep, moist soil and shelter. Suitable for large water gardens, as it can grow to over 3 × 4.5 m (10 × 15 ft).

Hosta 'Halcyon'

Hosta
An essential foliage perennial for moist soil and semi-shade, with a wide range of cultivars producing broad, lanceolate, glaucous leaves in shades varying from blue to lime green, often with creamy stripes or margins. Note that they are equally prized by slugs and snails. *H. fortunei* 'Marginato-alba' has sage-green leaves with a broad white edge while the leaves of *H.f.* 'Albopicta' are lime-yellow with a darker green outer margin. *H. siebol-diana* is very handsome with 90 cm (3 ft) long, broad blue-grey leaves. Good as architectural features, in drifts for ground cover or as specimens in pots.

Nandina – Chinese sacred bamboo
N. domestica is a clump-forming, half-hardy shrub with delicate, feathery foliage on slender, vertical stems re-aching 1.2–1.8 cm (4–6 ft) and panicles of white flowers in summer. White fruits last through the winter. Must have shelter and rich, moist, well-drained soil.

Phormium
P. tenax. is a useful evergreen with a strong architectural form. It forms tall, erect clumps of leathery strap-shaped leaves up to 2.7 m (9 ft) long and 10 cm (4 in) wide. *P.t.* 'Pur-pureum' has bronze-purple foliage which associates well with grey and silver plants; *P.t.* 'Variegatum' is striped with green and yellow. Needs sun and moist soil with some protection in winter.

Phyllostachys nigra – Black bamboo
A tall, elegant bamboo with shiny, hard, black stems and narrow rustling leaves. Must have a sheltered position and moist, well-drained soil. Grows to 2.4–3 m (8–10 ft).

Rodgersia
A group of hardy herbaceous perennials with strong foliage forms. *R. aesculifolia* has glossy, bronzed leaves resembling a horse chestnut, with plumes of tiny flowers in midsummer, and measures 0.9–1.8 m (3–6 ft).

R. podophylla has a similar form but the leaves are green, and the plant only grows to a height of 0.9–1.2 m (3–4 ft). They need moist soil and semi-shade.

Grey & Silver

Achillea – Yarrow
A family of hardy herbaceous perennials needing sun and well-drained soil.

A. argentea, 15 × 30 cm (6 × 12 in) silver cushion of narrow leaves, white flowers in early summer, good for border edging.

A. 'Peter Davies 166', 23 × 25 cm (9 × 10 in), finely cut grey leaves, white flowers in summer.

A. taygetea, 50 × 45 cm (20 × 18 in), silver-green ferny foliage, prolific soft yellow flowers good for drying. Hardy.

Anaphalis – Pearl everlasting
White woolly hairs cover the lanceolate grey leaves giving them a silvery appearance. Clusters of ivory-white starry flowers, suitable for cutting and drying, appear in late summer. It tends to spread very quickly and is happy on all but the heaviest soils.

A. triplinervis grows to 30–45 cm

Anaphalis triplinervis

(12–18 in). With larger flat flower heads, *A. yedoensis* reaches a height of 60 cm (2 ft).

Artemisia – Wormwood

A. absinthium 'Lambrook Silver'; very hardy sun-loving shrub, to 90 cm (3 ft), finely incised shining silver leaves. Mimosa-like flowers, summer. Cut back hard after flowering.

A. arborescens; tender but most beautiful of the species, grows to 90 cm (3 ft) or more in very sheltered spots, with foliage like shimmering silver-white filaments. Prune to keep in shape.

A. nutans 'Silver Queen'; hardy and good on clay soil, with willow-like, narrow grey leaves, H 60 cm (2 ft). Flimsy-looking so best planted in groups.

A. 'Powis Castle' is hardy, compact and pewter coloured with very few flowers.

A. stelleriana; hardy and tougher looking than others of the species, tolerant of coastal conditions and of some damp and shade, 45 × 60 cm (18 × 24 in).

Ballota

B. pseudodictamnus is a low-growing, branching, hardy shrub for full sun; 60 × 60 cm (24 × 24 in). Heart-shaped, apple-green leaves turn white and woolly through summer. Tiny white, purple-spotted flowers borne in whorls in midsummer.

Centaurea

C. gymnocarpa 'Colchester White' forms a mound of beautiful, down-turning, fern-like, silvery foliage, 45 × 45 cm (18 × 18 in). Remove flowering stem, best for summer bedding in a dry site.

Convolvulus

C. cneorum; exquisitely beautiful half-hardy shrub, with narrow leaves covered in silky down, catching light with shimmering iridescence. Pure white flowers opening from pink buds cover the plant throughout summer. Full sun; provide extra grit for drainage, cannot stand cold, wet soil; 45 × 45 cm (18 × 18 in).

Convolvulus cneorum

Cynara – Cardoon

C. cardunculus, hardy perennial; huge, dramatic, curving, blue-grey leaves with deeply cut jagged edges and purple, thistle flowers on 2.4 m (8 ft) stems in late summer. More decorative than the edible artichoke, *C. scolymous*.

Eryngium – Sea holly

E. maritimum; hardy perennial, 45 cm (18 in), needing sun and good drainage. Broad prickly silver-green leaves below metallic blue teazle-shaped flowers in late summer. *E. alpinum* has dark blue-green, heart-shaped leaves with steel-blue flowers and bracts. Both good for salt air.

Festuca

F. orina glauca is an exquisite, fine blue grass growing in thick tufts. Full sun and light soil; 15–25 cm (6–10 in). Good for edging.

Helichrysum

H. angustifolium; 60 × 60 cm (24 × 24 in), reliable small shrub with bright silver, needle-like leaves smelling strongly of curry. Encourage new growth by snipping off unpleasant yellow flowers. Good in winter. *H.a.* 'Mini' is a sweet miniature version.

H. italicum; 30 × 30 cm (12 × 12 in), good for dwarf hedging with bright silver foliage. Not hardy, must have well-drained soil. Trim regularly to keep in shape.

H. petiolatum; tender trailing plant with round, felted grey leaves. Good for window boxes, tubs and hanging baskets.

Helleborus

H. argutifolius; 60 × 60 cm (24 × 24 in), evergreen perennial with thick, spiny, grey-green leaves. Pale green cup-shaped flowers, up to 5 cm (2 in) across, appear in clusters on 60 cm (2 ft) stems in early spring. Needs shade and rich, loamy soil. Wonderful for winter interest in the border.

Lavandula – Lavender

L. angustifolia, the English lavender measures up to 90 × 90 cm (36 × 36 in), has silver-grey leaves and blue flowers.

L. vera, Dutch lavender, 45 × 60 cm (18 × 24 in), is more compact with grey-green leaves and purplish flowers. Shorter growing and more compact, it is more suitable for low hedges and edging; 'Alba' and 'Nana Alba' have white flowers.

Macleaya – Plume poppy

M. cordata, an impressive hardy perennial with broad, deeply lobed leaves, grey underneath and slightly bronzy above, has plumes 90 cm (3 ft) high of tiny pearly flowers which appear above the foliage in late summer. H to 2.4 m (8 ft) and very invasive.

Onopordum – Scotch thistle

O. acanthium is a dramatic, prickly, silvery leaved biennial. For the back of a border as it reaches 1.8 m (6 ft) high. Good for flower arranging.

Santolina – Cotton lavender

S. chamaecyparissus, 45 × 60 cm (18 × 24 in), appears as a mound of densely packed, finely incised silvery, woolly leaves on felted stems. Very hardy, excellent for hedging; prune regularly to maintain shape. *S.c. nana* has pungent foliage; miniature version, 30 × 45 cm (12 × 18 in).

Senecio

S. maritima is a good annual for summer bedding, 60 cm (2 ft). *S.m.* 'Diamond' has deeply divided white leaves; 'Silver Dust' has felted, densely packed, ferny foliage.

S. laxifolius grows as a vigorous shrub to 1.2 m (4 ft) or more with white felted leaves and lax habit. Prune in spring to keep in shape and cut off yellow daisy-like flowers.

Stachys lanata

Stachys – Lamb's lugs

S. lanata is one of the best-loved grey plants with leaves covered in thick white 'fur' and spikes of purple flowers, 30–45 cm (12–18 in). 'Silver Carpet' is a compact, non-flowering form. Remove withering leaves regularly to maintain silvery appearance.

Tanacetum

T. haradjanii makes dense, creeping mats of silver filigree foliage, perfect for ground cover. Needs gritty soil and full sun.

Teucrium – Tree germander

T. fruticans is a half-hardy shrub with aromatic grey-green leaves, 1.2–1.5 m (4–5 ft). Best against a warm, sheltered wall.

Water Gardens

Aruncus sylvester – Goat's beard

Hardy herbaceous perennial carrying large leaves with a mass of small leaflets from which appear tall branching plumes of creamy flowers; H 1.2–1.8 m (4–6 ft). *A.s.* 'Kneiffii' has more deeply cut leaflets and grows to 60 cm (2 ft). Needs partial shade and deep, moist soil.

Astilbe

Hardy herbaceous perennials with dark green, deeply divided foliage and plumes of feathery flowers. Must have permanently moist soil, sun or shade.

A. × arendsii 'White Gloria'; feathery foliage and pyramidal panicles of bloom in late summer; H 60 cm (2 ft). *A. grandis*; dark green leaves with 90 cm (3 ft) spreading panicles in mid-summer; H 1.2–1.8 m (4–6 ft).

Camassia quamash

Large, edible bulbs, producing flower stems, covered at the top by large, white star-like flowers. Heavy, moist soil; H 75 cm (30 in).

Cardiocrinum giganteum

Cardiocrinum giganteum – Giant Himalayan lily

Bulb producing huge, bell-shaped blooms in later summer. H 1.8–3 m (6–10 ft). *See also* 'Bulbs'.

Filipendula hexapetala – Dropwort

Hardy herbaceous perennial with deeply cut, fern-like leaves with drifts of creamy panicles of tiny flowers in summer. Moist soil, part sun or shade, H 60–90 cm (2–3 ft).

Glyceria maxima – Great water grass

A vigorous deciduous perennial, equally happy planted directly in water or at the pool margin. *G.m.* 'Variegata' has leaves striped with white and yellow, less invasive, H 0.75–1.2 m (30–48 in).

Heracleum mantegazzianum

A short-lived biennial with 90 cm (3 ft) long coarse leaves. Stout stems are topped with clusters of tiny flowers up to 45 cm (18 in) wide in late summer. Suitable only for large, wild situations with moist soil, sun or part shade; H 3–3.6 m (10–12 ft).

Houttuynia cordata

Hardy herbaceous perennial for wet soil or shallow water. Heart-shaped, metallic blue foliage with erect cones of white bracts, all with a tangy scent. *H.c.* 'Plena' is a double form. Can be invasive; H 30–45 cm (12–18 in).

Houttuynia cordata 'Chameleon'

Iris

I. laevigata is a true water species which will grow in water up to 15 cm (6 in) deep or at the poolside, deciduous. *I.l.* 'Alba' is pure white and *I.l.* 'Monstrosa' is white with blue blotches, early summer. H 45–60 cm (18–24 in).

I. sibirica is a branching form to be cultivated in the pool margin about 15 cm (6 in) above water level. *I.s.* 'White Swirl' produces pure white flowers, standing 90 cm (3 ft) high.

Juncus – Bog rush

Hardy evergreen water plant for unusual foliage effect. *J. effusus* 'Spiralis' forms itself into curious spirals and corkscrews up to 45 cm (18 in) high.

Leucojum – Summer snowflake

Bulbs producing green-tipped flowers closely resembling snowdrops, suitable for moist soil and dappled shade at the pool margin. Leave undisturbed once planted. *L. aestivum* 'Gravetye Giant' has 2.5 cm (1 in) long flowers in spring; H 60 cm (2 ft). *L. vernum* is smaller, flowering earlier in the year, standing only 20 cm (8 in).

Lysichiton

L. camtschatcense is a hardy herbaceous perennial for wet ground at the poolside. It produces huge white, arum-like flowers with prominent green spathes in spring, followed by massive glaucous leaves; H 60–90 cm (2–3 ft).

Nymphaea 'Odorata Alba'

Nymphaea – Waterlily

Indispensable for natural or ornamental ponds, there are a number of beautiful forms. Hardy forms include: 'Gladstoniana', large, water depth of 1.2–1.8 m (4–6 ft), pure white flowers, 20–25 cm (8–10 in) across; 'Helvola', miniature, water depth 15–30 cm (6–12 in), free flowering cream blooms, 5 cm (2 in) across; *N.* 'Marliacea Albida', medium producing many leaves, water depth 60–90 cm (2–3 ft), pure white flowers, 10–15 cm (4–6 in) across.

Primula

P. denticulata 'Alba' is a vigorous perennial, producing globes of white flowers on thick stems in spring, H 30 cm (12 in). *P. japonica*, 'Postford White' is a short-lived candelabra form flowering in early summer, also measuring 30 cm (12 in).

Conservatory

Abutilon

A. × *hybridum* 'Boule de Neige' is a branching shrub with pendent flowers throughout summer. Cut back by half in early spring. H 1.8–2.4 m (6–8 ft).

Aristolochia – Dutchman's pipe

A. elegans is a fast-growing, unusual evergreen climber with heart-shaped leaves fascinating hooded, maroon flowers speckled with white in late summer. H 3 m (10 ft).

Bougainvillea

A vigorous deciduous climber with large, long-lasting, papery bracts formed on the current year's growth. The white form of *B.* × *buttiana* has a rather ephemeral appearance compared with its more familiar and showy pink cousins, while *B. spectabilis* has panicles of much smaller pink-tinged bracts.

Dry off plants in winter, cut back main growths in February and spur prune all laterals to within 5 cm (2 in) of the main stem. Good drainage and plenty of sunshine are essential. H to 4.5–6 m (15–20 ft).

Camellia

This is surely one of the most beautiful of the flowering shrubs with huge, waxy blooms in winter and early spring set off by glossy dark green foliage. Although perfectly suitable for outdoor culture in milder climates, white-flowering forms benefit especially from protection from rain and scorching winter winds both of which tend to discolour the blooms.

C. japonica 'White Swan' is a pure white single form with a prominent boss of yellow stamens, and 'Lady Vansittart' is a delicate, semi-double with a subtle pale pink stripe. Grow them in ericaceous compost which should never be allowed to dry out. Best suited to an unheated conservatory with protection from frost. H to 1.8–2.4 m (6–8 ft).

Campanula – Italian bell flower
This is a lovely plant for a hanging basket; produces masses of pure white bell-shaped flowers throughout the summer. Regular dead-heading is a must; water frequently and feed with a high potash fertiliser. H 30 cm (12 in).

Citrus
The combination of fruits – both edible and decorative – and glossy, evergreen foliage make this group of plants irresistible. Choose from lemons, oranges or limes, kumquats or calamondins; though the fruits are not white, the heavily scented blossoms are and will usually be showing at the same time as the previous seasons fruits are ripening. They prefer cool winter temperatures and benefit hugely from being taken outside during the summer months. Water and syringe frequently and feed throughout the spring and summer with a high potash fertiliser. H 0.9–2.4 m (3–8 ft).

Clerodendrum
C. thomsoniae is a fast-growing, evergreen climber producing white lantern-shaped flowers with a red corolla, in pendulous panicles throughout the summer. H 3.6 m (12 ft).

Datura – Angels' trumpets
D. cornigera 'Knightii' is a dramatic-looking shrub originating in Mexico. Growing to 2.4 m (8 ft), with a similar

Datura 'Grand Marnier'

spread, it produces huge, pendulous blooms of a waxy texture and heavily scented. Over-hot conditions allow red spider mite to proliferate so syringe daily in summer. The sap of this plant is poisonous. Cut back hard in February to promote bushy new growth.

Gardenia
Heavily perfumed, double-formed waxy blooms are freely produced on this evergreen shrub. The long-lasting flowers open white and fade to a rich clotted cream, and are suitable for table decorations or bouquets. They need plenty of moisture, both at the roots and in the surrounding air. Bud drop will usually indicate dryness.

G. jasminoides 'Veitchiana' is one of the largest flowering forms, producing blooms 7 cm (3 in) across. Grown in a pot, this plant will usually reach a height and spread of 0.9–1.2 m (3–4ft) but it should be lightly pruned in winter to maintain a dense, bushy shape.

Hibiscus
H. rosa-sinensis is a handsome, evergreen shrub from China producing masses of extravagant, short-lived blooms up to 12 cm (5 in) across, opening in the morning and dying at night. White forms have a central blotch of deep red. They need plenty of sun and moist roots. Prune hard in spring to encourage bushy new growth and prolific flowering. H 1.2–1.8 m (4–6 ft).

Jasminum – Jasmine
A vigorous, twining climber with delicate evergreen foliage and clusters of small, tubular flowers with a very sweet scent.

J. polyanthum makes masses of pink-tinged blooms in winter and early spring, attaining a height of 3 m (10 ft) or more.

J. officinale 'Grandiflorum' has larger, pure white flowers in late summer and a more shrubby habit.

While these prefer cool, moist conditions, *J. sambac* with its singly produced, highly fragrant blooms, fading from white to purple, prefers humid warmth.

Leptospermum – Tea tree
L. scoparium is a bushy shrub with greyish, needle-like leaves and starry, black-centred, white flowers carried profusely in early summer.

Lonicera – Giant honeysuckle
L. hildebrandiana is a vigorous, evergreen climber from Burma with delicately fragrant, tubular, white and yellow flowers, up to 15 cm (6 in) long in later summer.

Nerium – Oleander
N. oleander is a graceful shrub; makes masses of tall stems of narrow, leathery leaves topped by clusters of single or double, pure white or creamy blooms throughout the summer. Water freely in summer but allow to dry in winter and prune back by about one-third. All parts of the plant are extremely poisonous. H 1.2–1.8 m (4–6 ft).

Orchid
Of the numerous species of orchids available, only a few are suitable for general cultivation. There are beautiful white forms to be found amongst Cymbidiums and Phaelenopsis which are easy to cultivate and are available from florists or garden centres.

Passiflora – Passion flower
These vigorous evergreen climbers reach heights of up to 6 m (20 ft) and produce a mass of strangely formed flowers 7–10 cm (3–4 in) across in summer.

P. edulis has white petals with a purple corona, producing edible fruits which ripen in autumn. The 10 cm (4 in) flowers of *P. quadrangularis* are white, flushed purple with a dramatic corona of white and purple wavy filaments; its large yellow fruits seldom set under glass. Thin out plants in early spring.

Pittosporum
P. tobira is a handsome evergreen shrub with leathery greyish green leaves reaching a height of 2.4 m (8 ft). Dense clusters of tiny, heavily scented creamy flowers occur in spring. *P. tobira* 'Nana' is a good prostrate form, suitable for underplanting and 'Variegatum' has silvery streaked foliage. Best for cool conservatories.

Plumbago
P. capensis is best known as a blue-flowering evergreen shrubby climber but an equally delightful white form is available which produces clusters of tubular blooms through the summer. Cut back after flowering, shortening growths by two-thirds. H 2.4–3 m (8–10 ft).

Stephanotis
One of the most highly prized white flowers, *S. floribunda* is a glossy leaved, evergreen climber producing heavily scented, tubular waxy blooms right through the summer. They need a warm and humid environment with dryer conditions in winter. H 4.5 m (15 ft).

Stephanotis floribunda

Sparmannia – Indoor lime
A marvellous foliage shrub for a cool greenhouse, *S. africana* reaches a height of 2.4 m (8 ft), its huge, lime-green translucent leaves covered in downy hair. Small but attractive white flowers with a prominent boss of yellow stamens appear in early summer. Leaves discolour in winter so prune back heavily to promote fresh growth in spring.

Trachelospermum
Good for a cool conservatory, *T. jasminoides* is an evergreen climber which will densely cover a wall. Masses of tiny, sweetly scented flowers are produced in summer. Thin out in spring if required. H 3–3.6 m (10–12 ft).

FURTHER READING

Bird, Richard, *Flowering Trees and Shrubs*, Ward Lock, 1989
Boisset, Caroline, *The Vertical Garden*, Mitchell Beazley, 1988
Bown, Deni, *Alba*, Unwin Hyman, 1989
Chatto, Beth, *The Dry Garden*, J. M. Dent, 1981
Genders, Roy, *The Cottage Garden and the Old Fashioned Flowers*, Pelham Books, 1983
Hobhouse, Penelope, *Colour in Your Garden*, Collins, 1985
Jekyll, Gertrude, *Colour Schemes for the Flower Garden*, Antique Collectors Club
Kelly, John, *Foliage in Your Garden*, Frances Lincoln, 1988
Paul, Anthony and Rees, Yvonne, *The Water Garden*, Frances Lincoln, 1986
Tresidder, Jane, *Living Under Glass*, Thames & Hudson, 1986
Underwood, Mrs Desmond, *Grey and Silver Plants*, Collins, 1971
The RHS Gardeners' Encyclopedia of Plants and Flowers, Dorling Kindersley, 1989

INDEX

Page numbers in *italic* refer to the illustrations

ACKNOWLEDGEMENTS

The author and publisher would like to thank the following photographers and organizations for their permission to reproduce the photographs in this book:

Michael Boys 29, 42, 46, 47 left, 56 below, 57
The Garden Picture Library: Henk Dijkman 7, 49; Marijke Heuff 26–7, 39; John Neubauer 30 right; Jerry Pavia 35; Gary Rogers 33 above left; Ron Sutherland 10–11, 31; Steven Wooster 68 left, 80 left
W. Halliday FRPS 101 right
Jerry Harpur 2 (Chenies Manor, Bucks), 36 below (Designer Mrs McBurnie), 61 left (Kemerton Priory, Glos)
Jacqui Hurst 22, 28 right, 53, 65, 85 right, 87 left, 95 left
Andrew Lawson 1, 4–5, 6–7, 8, 9, 11, 12, 13, 14, 15, 17, 20, 21, 24, 25, 27, 28 left, 30 left, 32, 33 below left, 36 above, 37, 38, 40, 41, 44, 47 right, 48–9, 52, 60, 61 right, 64, 68 right, 69, 72, 76 left, 80 right, 82–3, 84, 85 left, 86, 87 right, 88, 89, 90, 91, 92, 93, 94, 95 right, 96, 97, 98, 99, 100, 101 left, 102, 103, 104, 105, 106, 107
Marston & Langinger 76 right
John Miller 19, 56 above, 73

Half-title page *Agapanthus* Ardernei hybrid
Title page Chenies Manor, Bucks
Contents *Tulipa* 'White Triumphator'
page 6–7 *Clematis flammula*
page 7 (inset) A white garden in Holland
page 10–11 *Hosta fortunei, H. f. albopicta, H. undulata univittata*
page 11 (inset) *Helleborus orientalis*
page 26–7 A topiary enclosed garden
page 27 (inset) Garden ornament and statuary
page 48–9 *Anthemis punctata cupaniana*
page 49 (inset) A formal white garden
page 82–3 *Eryginium giganteum*
page 83 (inset) *Romneya coulteri*